CASH IN A FLASH

UNLOCKING PASSIVE INCOME WITH MINIMAL EFFORT

By Brian C Eby

Table of Contents

PART II SETUP AND LAUNCH

PREFACE

In a world increasingly dominated by digital transactions and complex business models, a timeless allure exists in the cash-based business. It's a realm where simplicity meets opportunity, offering a tangible sense of control and immediacy in every transaction. This book is born from a fascination with such businesses, specifically focusing on three enduring examples: vending machines, car washes, and. These enterprises, often overlooked in the grand narrative of entrepreneurship, embody the essence of cash-based commerce. They offer simplicity, scalability, and a direct connection to people's everyday needs. This guide is a comprehensive exploration of how to develop, open, and operate a cash-based business from its conceptual stages to a self-sustaining entity, using these three models as the foundation for broader lessons in entrepreneurship. The benefits of cash-based businesses, such as immediate revenue and reduced risk of fraud, make them a viable and attractive option even in a digital age.

The appeal of cash transactions lies not just in their simplicity but in the tactile interaction they involve—an exchange of value that is immediate and unambiguous. In an era where digital payments often mask the intricacies of financial flows, cash brings us back to the basics of commerce. This foundational principle makes vending machines and car washes perfect subjects for this book. Both are ubiquitous, yet they operate on an increasingly rare model. They provide essential or convenient services in a straightforward, pay-as-you-go manner. But don't let the simplicity deceive you; the journey from a blank sheet of paper to a profitable cash-based business is complex, challenging, and deeply rewarding.

This book is a practical guide that aims to lead the process of starting a cash-based business. It is for the entrepreneurs who see potential in the most everyday transactions. It's for the pragmatists who seek a solid, step-by-step blueprint to turn that potential into reality. And it's for the curious minds fascinated by how a simple concept can evolve into a thriving business. By focusing on vending machines, car washes, food trucks, and laundromats, I delve into the universal principles of cash-based businesses—market research, customer behavior, location scouting, financial planning, and more. These principles apply broadly, as the author wants to provide valuable insights from these pages regardless of the specific business you dream of starting.

Why vending machines and car washes, specifically? They are accessible. They require relatively low initial investments compared to other ventures and are ripe with opportunities for innovation and growth. They are scalable, allowing entrepreneurs to start small and expand gradually. Most importantly, they serve as ideal learning platforms for the broader lessons of entrepreneurship—lessons about identifying opportunities, understanding your customers, managing operations efficiently, and scaling responsibly. The unique challenges and opportunities presented by vending machines and car washes make them excellent case studies for understanding the principles of cash-based businesses, which can be applied to a wide range of other ventures.

This book is structured to walk you through every phase of building a cash-based business. It starts with narrowing down your options and focusing on a single business concept, guiding you through market analysis, planning, and securing financing. From there, it covers the practicalities of location, design, construction, and operation setup. The narrative then transitions into the day-to-day routines of running your business, including maintenance, financial management, and customer service. Finally, it addresses growth and adaptation, offering strategies for expanding your enterprise and ensuring its long-term viability in an ever-changing market. With its comprehensive coverage, this book ensures you are well-equipped and prepared for every step of your entrepreneurial journey.

Each section is designed not just to inform but to inspire action. The chapters contain actionable advice, real-world examples, and practical tools to aid decision-making. Whether you're navigating the complexities of financial projections or the specifics of equipment selection, you'll find detailed guidance and insights drawn from the front lines of cash-based entrepreneurship. This emphasis on practical tools and real-world examples ensures you feel supported and guided in your entrepreneurial journey.

Remember, this book is more than just a manual; it's a companion in your entrepreneurial soul. It reflects a belief in the power of simplicity, the value of hard work, and the potential of a good idea well executed. The road from concept to successful operation is seldom straight, but with the proper knowledge and tools, it's a path filled with potential for personal and financial growth. This book provides valuable insights and practical tools to apply to a wide range of cash-based businesses, regardless of the specific business you dream of starting.

So, welcome to a deep dive into the world of vending machines and car washes—a starting point for a broader exploration of what it means to build a business that's both simple in concept and rich in opportunity. This book is your first step toward turning the straightforward act of a cash transaction into a foundation for lasting success.

Part I
Foundation And Planning

CHAPTER 1

UNDERSTANDING THE CASH-BASED BUSINESS

In an era where digital and credit transactions increasingly dominate the market, the concept of a cash-based business might seem quaint, if not outright archaic. Yet, this traditional mode of operation remains viable, profoundly lucrative, and relevant. The appeal of cash transactions is timeless, offering a simplicity and immediacy that digital transactions struggle to match. This chapter delves into the allure of cash transactions, explores the resilience of cash-based business models, and examines why certain enterprises, like vending machines and car washes, thrive under this model.

The Appeal of Cash Transactions

Cash transactions represent the most ancient form of commerce, a direct value exchange between two parties. In a world increasingly cluttered with intermediary processes, fees, and delayed settlements, cash stands out for its simplicity and immediacy. Cash transactions are final; they require no third-party verification and incur no processing delays. This anonymity and simplicity are highly valued in an age where privacy concerns and digital tracking are omnipresent. However, I must note that most vending machines and car washes now accept credit cards as a form of payment.

Cash transactions are universally accessible. They require no technological infrastructure beyond an electrical outlet and a secure, safe place to store the cash. This accessibility makes cash-based businesses especially appealing in areas with limited digital payment penetration or demographics that are less comfortable with technology. Additionally, the overhead of credit card fees can be prohibitive for small transactions, making cash the economically sensible choice for businesses and customers.

Why Cash-Based Business Models Persist

Despite the rise of digital payments, cash-based business models persist and, in many niches, thrive. The reasons are manifold. These models often operate in sectors where small, frequent transactions are the norm, such as snack vending or car cleaning services. Here, the efficiency and low transaction cost of cash are unbeatable advantages.

Cash-based businesses also enjoy financial flexibility and liquidity, which is particularly attractive to small and medium entrepreneurs. The immediacy of cash flow allows for rapid response to operational needs and opportunities without the delays inherent to credit settlements or the unpredictability of digital payment systems.

Furthermore, cash transactions foster a different type of customer relationship. They encourage impulse buying, given their straightforwardness and the psychological effect of parting with physical money, which can feel less significant than swiping a card. This psychological aspect can be particularly leveraged in businesses like vending machines, where the impulse purchase of snacks or drinks constitutes a significant portion of sales.

The Enduring Success of Vending Machines, Laundromats, and Car Washes

Vending machines, laundromats, car washes, and other cash-based businesses not only exemplify the enduring success of cash-based models but also inspire their potential. With their wide variety of offerings, from snacks and beverages to electronics and cosmetics, vending machines cater to immediate consumer needs with unparalleled convenience. Their ability to operate 24/7 without direct supervision makes them highly efficient cash generators. The simplicity of the transaction—a customer inserts cash and selects a product—minimizes operational complexity and maximizes accessibility and convenience.

On the other hand, car washes capitalize on the necessity of vehicle maintenance. Service customers are often willing to pay in cash, especially for small discounts or quick and additional services. The car wash model allows for various cash-based transaction points, from self-service bays to full-service operations. These can include the initial payment for the wash, additional services like waxing or vacuuming, and even tips for the staff, appealing to a broad customer base with different needs and spending habits.

In the following chapters, we will explore how to harness the potential of cash-based businesses, starting with the crucial first step: generating a viable business concept. Through a blend of strategic planning, market analysis, and an understanding of customer behavior, entrepreneurs can lay the foundation for a successful venture in cash-based commerce.

Vending machines, car washes, food trucks, and laundromats benefit from the physicality of their transactions. Inserting coins or bills and receiving a tangible product or service in return has a certain satisfaction that digital transactions struggle to replicate. This tangibility, coupled with the immediate fulfillment of customer needs, forms the core appeal of these businesses.

Understanding the dynamics of cash-based businesses is crucial for entrepreneurs looking to venture into this traditional yet surprisingly dynamic segment of the economy. The resilience of these models lies in their simplicity, accessibility, and the directness of their transactions. Vending machines and car washes are prime examples of how cash-based operations can successfully navigate the modern economic landscape, combining the timeless appeal of cash transactions with the operational efficiency and customer appeal necessary for business success. This simplicity and accessibility should reassure you of the potential of these businesses and instill confidence in your entrepreneurial journey.

CHAPTER 2

GENERATING YOUR BUSINESS CONCEPT

A successful cash-based business begins with a foundational step: generating a viable, innovative business concept. This chapter is dedicated to guiding aspiring entrepreneurs through the intricate process of creativity, market analysis, and concept development. It focuses on establishing a solid foundation for their vending machine or car wash business. It will delve into identifying opportunities in the market, conducting thorough research, and fine-tuning a business concept that not only fulfills a market need but also aligns with the entrepreneur's passions and capabilities.

Identifying Opportunities

The first step in generating a business concept is to identify opportunities in the market. This involves observing consumer behaviors, understanding market trends, and identifying gaps in the current offerings. For vending machines, this could mean spotting locations with high foot traffic but limited access to quick snack or drink options. For car washes, it might involve recognizing an area with a high density of vehicle owners but a shortage of convenient, efficient car cleaning services.

To identify these opportunities, entrepreneurs must immerse themselves in the target market, engage with potential customers, and conduct competitive analyses. This process can reveal insights into what customers truly value and what is currently missing. It's also essential to consider emerging trends, such as the growing emphasis on eco-friendly products and services, which can offer new niches and opportunities for differentiation.

Before proceeding with this chapter, let's take a moment to identify what types of cash-based businesses exist beyond the three examples we have chosen to focus on in this book.

Here's a list of types of businesses that commonly operate on a cash basis:

- Food trucks and food stalls at fairs and festivals
- Second-hand stores and flea markets
- Barbershops
- Nail and beauty salons
- Tattoo shops
- Convenience stores
- Bakeries, cafes, and coffee shops
- Ice cream trucks
- Taxi services
- Parking lots
- Artisan, craft, or handmade goods vendors
- Street and subway performers
- Farmers' markets and roadside produce stands
- Bicycle repair shops
- Small repair services (e.g., shoe repair, key cutting)
- Massage therapists

Independent fitness trainers and instructors

Pet groomers

Tailors and seamstresses

Housekeeping and cleaning services

This is only a partial list. Nearly countless other businesses are, or can be, cash-based, depending on how the owner wants to structure and operate them.

Research and Market Analysis

Once potential opportunities have been identified, the next step is to investigate them further through research and market analysis. This phase is critical for validating the viability of your business concept and refining it to match the market's needs better. Market analysis is not just a step; it's a tool that will keep you informed and prepared for the challenges and opportunities in the market.

Market analysis for a vending machine or car wash business involves examining several vital areas:

- **Demographics and Psychographics**: Understanding your target customers' characteristics, preferences, and motives.
- **Market Size and Potential**: Estimating the number of potential customers and the market's overall revenue potential.
- **Competition**: Identify businesses that offer similar products or services and examine their strengths and weaknesses.
- **Location Analysis**: Evaluating the strategic importance of location for your business and identifying potential sites for your vending machines or car wash.

Remember, your research should be thorough and data-driven, utilizing primary sources (such as surveys and customer interviews) and secondary sources (such as industry reports and academic studies). This will give you the confidence to make informed decisions about your business strategy.

Fine-Tuning the Business Concept

With a solid understanding of the market and its opportunities, you are now in a position to fine-tune your business concept. This involves making strategic decisions about the specific products or services you will offer, how to differentiate yourself from competitors, and how to deliver value to your customers.

For a vending machine business, this might mean specializing in healthy snack options or high-tech vending machines that accept digital payments and offer interactive shopping experiences. For a car wash, differentiation could come from offering eco-friendly washing methods, subscription services, or additional convenience features such as mobile booking.

The key to fine-tuning your business concept is to align it with your market research, ensuring that it not only stands out from the competition but also addresses your target customers' specific needs and preferences. It's also important to consider your concept's operational and financial aspects, ensuring that it is feasible to implement and capable of generating a healthy profit.

Case Studies: Successes and Lessons Learned

To illustrate the process of generating and refining a business concept, let's look at brief case studies of successful vending machine and car wash businesses:

> **Vending Machine Business**: A successful entrepreneur identified an opportunity to offer organic, locally sourced snacks and beverages in vending machines located in office buildings and fitness centers. By focusing on health-conscious consumers and

leveraging the trend towards healthier eating, the business was able to differentiate itself from traditional vending machines offering processed snacks and sodas.

Car Wash Business: Recognizing the growing demand for eco-friendly services, a car wash entrepreneur developed a concept for a waterless car wash that uses environmentally friendly products and practices. The business appealed to environmentally conscious customers and offered a convenient mobile service that could clean cars at the customer's location.

Generating a viable business concept is a critical first step in creating a successful cash-based business. By identifying market opportunities, conducting thorough research and analysis, and fine-tuning the business concept to align with customer needs and market trends, entrepreneurs can lay a solid foundation for their venture. Whether it's a vending machine offering healthy snacks or an eco-friendly car wash, the key is developing an innovative, differentiated, and financially viable concept. With a well-defined business concept, entrepreneurs are well-positioned to move forward to the next phase: developing a detailed business plan.

CHAPTER 3

DEVELOPING YOUR BUSINESS PLAN

Creating a detailed business plan is a pivotal step for any aspiring entrepreneur. It serves as a blueprint for your vending machine or car wash business, outlining your vision, objectives, strategies, and the financial forecasts that underpin your venture's potential success. This chapter will guide you through each critical component of a comprehensive business plan, ensuring a solid foundation to secure financing, attract investors, and guide your business to operational success.

Writing A Business Plan: Step-by-Step

Here is a very rudimentary outline of a business plan, followed by details on what needs to be addressed in the business plan:

Executive Summary

Introduction to the Business Plan

- Overview of the vending machine or car wash business concept.

- The mission statement and objectives of the business.
- A brief introduction to the founders and their backgrounds.

Business Description

- Detailed description of the business, including the type (vending machines, car wash, etc), the services offered, and the unique value proposition.
- Analysis of the business model: How will your business make money, focusing on cash transactions?
- Vision for the business's future growth and direction.

Market Analysis

- Overview of the industry, including current trends and growth projections.
- Target market identification: demographics, psychographics, and purchasing behaviors.
- Competitive analysis: Identify direct and indirect competitors, their strengths and weaknesses, and your business's competitive advantage.

Marketing and Sales Strategy

- Marketing plan: How you will attract and retain customers. Include strategies for pricing, promotions, advertising, and distribution.
- Sales strategy: Sales channels and tactics to drive revenue. For vending machines, this could include location strategy for car washes, service packages, and loyalty programs.

Operations Plan

- Describe the operational workflow, including sourcing supplies, inventory management, and customer service processes.
- Details on the location, facilities, and equipment needed for your business, including scalability and future expansion considerations.
- Information on suppliers and partners, highlighting any existing agreements or negotiations.

Financial Plan

- Overview of the startup costs, including detailed breakdowns for equipment, location acquisition, and initial inventory for vending machines or car wash supplies.
- Revenue projections for the first one to three years, with assumptions based on market analysis and marketing strategy.
- Break-even analysis to determine when the business will likely become profitable.
- Information on funding requirements: How much capital is needed to start and sustain the business until it becomes profitable, and potential sources of funding (loans, investments, grants).

The Introductory Section

Executive Summary

The executive summary is the gateway to your business plan, offering a concise overview of the most compelling aspects of your business venture. For a vending machine or car wash business, it highlights the uniqueness of the concept, the financial promise it holds, and the strategic direction intended by the founders. This section must capture the essence of the business, enticing potential investors or lenders to delve deeper into the plan.

Introduction to the Business Plan

Embarking on a journey to establish a cash-based business, whether through vending machines or car wash services, demands a visionary idea and a strategic roadmap to bring that vision to fruition. The business plan, serving as this roadmap, charts a course from concept to operational success. It outlines how the business will operate, attract customers, generate revenue, and scale over time. The introduction sets the stage, providing a snapshot of the business's core objectives and the entrepreneurial spirit driving its inception, clearly emphasizing the strategic roadmap.

Business Description

At the heart of every successful venture is a business model that effectively meets customer needs while ensuring profitability. For cash-based businesses like vending machines and car washes, the appeal lies in their straightforward transaction model and the immediate value they offer customers. This section delves into the specifics of the proposed business, detailing the services offered, the target market, and, most importantly, the unique advantages that set it apart from competitors. It also casts a vision for the future, outlining aspirations for growth, expansion, and evolution in response to market demands.

Market Analysis

A thorough understanding of the market landscape is crucial for tailoring your business to meet the most pressing needs of your target audience. This analysis covers the vending machine and car wash industries' size, trends, and potential for growth. It involves a deep dive into identifying your customers, what drives their purchasing decisions, and how your business can fulfill their needs better than the competition. Equally important is the competitive analysis, offering insights into how similar businesses have succeeded or failed and the niche your business aims to occupy within this competitive framework.

Building on this Chapter

The next step would be to continue building this chapter according to your requirements, focusing on the competition, marketing and sales strategies, operations plan, and financial projections. Each of these sections requires detailed development and a detailed and concise explanation. The outline for these is included in the outline a couple of pages back and in Appendix A at the back of the book.

CHAPTER 4

SECURING FINANCING

Securing financing is a crucial step in launching your cash-based business. Whether you want to start a vending machine empire or open a state-of-the-art car wash, finding the proper financial backing will turn your dreams into reality. This chapter will explore various financing options, how to prepare funding pitches, and strategies to make your business an attractive investment.

Understanding Your Financing Needs

Before seeking financing options, it's vital to understand your funding needs clearly. This section will guide you through assessing the startup costs associated with your business, including purchasing equipment, securing a location, and initial operating expenses. We'll also discuss the importance of protecting your cash flow to determine how much capital you'll need to cover expenses until your business becomes profitable.

Financing Options for Cash-Based Businesses

There are several paths to secure funding, each with advantages and drawbacks. We'll delve into traditional bank loans, highlighting their reliability and the stringent requirements and potential for high interest rates. Next, we'll explore Small Business Administration (SBA) loans, which offer more favorable terms for startups but require thorough documentation and a compelling business case.

Venture capital and angel investors present another avenue, especially for businesses with high growth potential. While these investors can provide significant capital and valuable business advice, they typically seek a portion of equity in return. We'll discuss attracting these investors and what to expect during the negotiation process.

Crowdfunding has emerged as a popular option, allowing entrepreneurs to raise small amounts of money from many people. This section will cover how to launch a successful crowdfunding campaign, including choosing the right platform, setting a funding goal, and marketing your campaign.

Preparing for the Pitch

Pitching investors or lenders is both an art and a science. This section will provide a step-by-step guide to crafting a compelling pitch, from developing a clear and concise presentation to anticipating questions and objections. We'll emphasize the importance of demonstrating your market knowledge, showcasing your business plan, and conveying your passion for the project.

Effective communication is critical to winning over investors. You'll learn storytelling techniques highlighting your business's potential impact, making it relatable and exciting. We'll also touch on the logistics of arranging pitch meetings, whether in person or virtually, and how to follow up effectively.

Mitigating Risks to Attract Financing

Investors and lenders are inherently risk-averse, so addressing potential risks upfront can make your business a more attractive investment. This section will focus on mitigating risks, such as securing insurance, establishing a solid management team, and presenting a realistic financial model with contingency plans.

We'll discuss the importance of transparency in acknowledging potential challenges and how you plan to address them. By showing that you have thought through the possible pitfalls and have a plan to manage them, you can build confidence in navigating the ups and downs of running a business.

Securing financing is a critical challenge for entrepreneurs, but it can be successfully overcome with the proper preparation and approach. This chapter has outlined the various financing options available to cash-based businesses and guided preparation for and execution of a successful pitch. By understanding your financing needs, exploring all funding avenues, and effectively communicating your vision and plans, you can secure the capital needed to launch and grow your vending machine or car wash business.

Dear Reader,

Thank you for reading "Cash In A Flash – Unlocking Passive Income with Minimal Effort."

As an independent author, your support means everything to me. If you enjoyed reading these pages, please consider leaving a review on the platform where you purchased it. Your feedback is invaluable and helps other readers discover this book.

Your honest review encourages me and helps me grow as a writer. Whether you loved it, found it thought-provoking, or have constructive criticism to share, I genuinely appreciate your input.

To leave a review, scan the QR code below to be taken to the Amazon page. Just a minute of your time and consideration are greatly appreciated.

Again, thank you for being a part of this literary adventure. I am honored.

Sincerely,

Brian

CHAPTER 5

LEGALITIES AND PERMITS

Navigating the legal landscape and securing the necessary permits is critical in establishing a cash-based business, such as vending machines or car washes. This chapter aims to guide you through the complexities of legal requirements, from choosing the proper business structure to understanding zoning laws and obtaining the permits and licenses essential for lawful operation.

Choosing the Best Business Structure

Selecting the appropriate legal structure for your business is foundational, affecting everything from your liability to how you pay taxes. For cash-based businesses, the options include sole proprietorship, partnership, limited liability company (LLC), and corporation. Each has advantages and disadvantages, particularly regarding personal asset protection, tax implications, and operational flexibility.

A sole proprietorship offers simplicity but does not provide a legal distinction between personal and business assets, which could be risky for business owners. Partnerships are similar but involve shared ownership and liability. LLCs offer a balance, providing legal separation of personal and business assets without the complexity of a corporation. While offering the most protection and fundraising options, corporations have significant regulatory and tax considerations.

Understanding Zoning Laws and Regulations

Zoning laws significantly impact where vending machines can be placed or where a car wash can be built. These regulations, determined by local municipalities, dictate land use for commercial purposes. Researching and complying with these laws is crucial to avoid costly fines and legal challenges.

For vending machines, considerations include restrictions on locations, such as schools or public parks, where certain types of products can be sold. Car washes face more stringent zoning considerations, often requiring specific environmental and water usage permits and adherence to noise regulations.

Obtaining Necessary Permits and Licenses

Securing the correct permits and licenses is essential for operating legally and avoiding operational disruptions. The process varies significantly between vending machines and car washes and across different locations.

Vending Machine Business:

- **Business License**: Almost universally required, this license formally recognizes your operation within a municipality.
- **Vendor's License**: Specific to vending operations, this may be required to sell certain types of products.
- **Health Permits**: Necessary if your vending machines sell perishable items, subject to local health department regulations.

Car Wash Business:

- **Business License**: As with vending machines, an essential legal requirement for operation.
- **Environmental Permits**: Depending on your location, you may need permits for water usage, waste disposal, and chemical handling.
- **Construction Permits**: Required if you're building a new facility or significantly modifying an existing one.

This section should include a step-by-step guide on researching the specific requirements in your area, tips for navigating the application process, and advice on maintaining compliance as your business grows and laws change.

Insurance: Protecting Your Assets

Insurance is an often overlooked but essential aspect of legal and financial protection. Types of insurance relevant to cash-based businesses include general liability insurance, property insurance, and, for car washes, specific policies covering environmental liability and customer vehicles.

General liability insurance protects against claims related to bodily injury or property damage caused by your business operations. Property insurance covers damage to your machines, equipment, and facilities from fire, theft, and other hazards. Given the nature of car wash operations, additional coverage for environmental liability (to protect against claims related to water usage and chemical handling) and policies covering damage to customer vehicles while in your care are also critical.

This section will guide you in evaluating your insurance needs and choosing the right policies and strategies for minimizing risk and liability through operational practices.

Understanding and navigating the legalities and permits required for your cash-based business is not just a regulatory hurdle but a foundation for long-term success and security. By carefully choosing your business structure, adhering to zoning laws, securing the necessary permits and licenses, and protecting your operation with the right insurance, you set your vending machine or car wash business on a path to lawful and profitable operation. This chapter has outlined the crucial steps and considerations in this process, offering a roadmap to compliance and peace of mind as you launch and grow your venture.

This section provides a substantive start to a comprehensive guide on managing the legal aspects of starting and running cash-based businesses like vending machines and car washes. To complete the chapter, we would expand each section with more detailed advice, incorporate case studies of businesses navigating these legal steps successfully, and provide a checklist for entrepreneurs to follow.

Continuing from the initial sections, let's delve deeper into the complexities of legalities and permits for cash-based businesses, expanding on the provided advice, integrating case studies, and concluding with a comprehensive checklist for entrepreneurs.

Expanding Legal Advice

Navigating Business Structures

Expanded Advice: Consider your immediate needs and long-term goals when selecting a business structure. A sole proprietorship might be suitable for a small, one-person operation but lacks protection against personal liability. An LLC, while more complex, offers significant flexibility and protection without the formalities of a corporation. Consult a legal advisor to choose the best structure for your situation, considering future growth and potential risks.

Case Study: Legal: Dan's Vending, initially a sole proprietorship, faced challenges as the business grew. Concerned about personal liability, especially given the physical placement of machines in high-traffic areas, John consulted a lawyer and decided to transition to an LLC. This move protected John's assets and enhanced the business's credibility with potential partners.

Mastering Zoning Laws and Regulations

Expanded Advice: Early engagement with local zoning boards and a thorough review of municipal codes are critical. Consider attending zoning board meetings to understand the board members' concerns and priorities. Proposing environmentally friendly practices can aid in securing approval for car washes, especially with stringent environmental regulations.

Case Study: EcoWash, an eco-friendly car wash, faced initial pushback from local zoning boards due to water usage concerns. By presenting a detailed plan that included water recycling and eco-friendly chemicals, along with community benefits like job creation, EcoWash secured the necessary permits and received local media attention, boosting its launch.

Securing Permits and Licenses

Expanded Advice: The process for obtaining permits and licenses can be lengthy and complicated. Start early and anticipate delays. Keep meticulous records of all interactions and submitted documents. Consider the need for multiple permits for vending machines if you plan to operate across different jurisdictions.

Case Study: VendTech, a startup deploying innovative vending machines, learned the importance of early planning when expanding to new cities. Each municipality had unique requirements, causing delays. By dedicating a team member to manage permits and liaise with city officials, VendTech streamlined its expansion process, avoiding previous setbacks.

Insurance: Beyond the Basics

Expanded Advice: Regularly review your insurance coverage to ensure it keeps pace with your business's growth. Consider adding umbrella policies for additional protection. Engage with an insurance broker who understands the vending machine or car wash industries and can advise on specialized coverage options.

Case Study: Splash & Dash, a car wash chain, suffered significant damage during a storm. While they had basic property insurance, they lacked coverage for business interruption, leading to financial strain. After this event, they worked with their insurance broker to add comprehensive coverage, protecting against future disruptions.

Checklist for Entrepreneurs

1. **Determine Your Business Structure:**
   - Consult a legal advisor to choose the structure that best suits your business.
   - Register your business according to your chosen structure.
2. **Understand Zoning Laws:**
   - Research local zoning laws applicable to your business location.
   - Attend zoning board meetings, if possible, to gather insights and network.
3. **Obtain Necessary Permits and Licenses:**
   - Create a list of required permits and licenses for your business and location.
   - Start the application process early, allowing for potential delays.
4. **Secure Adequate Insurance:**
   - Assess your business's insurance needs, considering all potential risks.

- Work with an insurance broker to find the best coverage options.

5. **Keep Records and Stay Informed:**
    - Maintain meticulous records of all legal documents, permits, and communications.
    - Regularly review and update your legal and insurance documents to reflect business changes or growth.
6. **Engage with the Community:**
    - Consider the community impact of your business, especially when dealing with zoning laws and regulations.
    - Engage in community service or local business associations to build goodwill and support.

By meticulously following these steps and learning from other businesses' experiences, you can navigate the legal landscape more effectively and set a solid foundation for your vending machine, food truck, or car wash business.

Part II
Setup And Launch

CHAPTER 6

FINANCIAL PLANNING AND BUDGETING

Financial planning and budgeting are crucial, particularly in cash-based operations like vending machines, car washes, and laundromats. These businesses face unique financial challenges and opportunities, including fluctuating daily cash flow, the need for regular equipment maintenance, and the potential for high upfront costs. Effective financial planning helps business owners navigate these challenges, ensuring stability, growth, and long-term profitability.

This chapter aims to equip business owners with the tools and strategies to create a robust financial plan, implement effective budgeting and forecasting techniques, secure necessary financing, manage cash flow efficiently, and regularly review and adjust financial plans. By mastering these aspects, business owners can build a solid financial foundation for their operations and make informed decisions that support sustainable growth.

Creating a Financial Plan

Critical Components of a Financial Plan Include:

Revenue Projections

Accurate revenue projections are the cornerstone of any financial plan. For cash-based businesses, this involves estimating future sales based on past performance, market trends, and customer behavior. Owners should consider factors such as seasonal fluctuations, local events, and changes in consumer preferences that might impact sales. A detailed sales forecast helps set realistic financial goals and planning for resource allocation.

Expense Budgeting

Managing expenses is critical for maintaining profitability. Expenses can be categorized into fixed costs like rent and insurance and variable costs like utilities and maintenance. It's essential to set realistic expense limits based on historical data and anticipated changes in the market. Tracking these costs allows business owners to identify areas to cut costs or reallocate funds more effectively.

Profitability Analysis

Understanding profitability is crucial for assessing the overall financial health of the business. This involves calculating gross profit margin (revenue minus the cost of goods sold) and net profit margin (gross profit minus all other expenses). Identifying the break-even point—where total revenue equals total costs—helps determine the minimum sales volume required to avoid losses. Profitability analysis guides pricing strategies and helps evaluate the financial viability of potential business expansions.

Budgeting and Forecasting Techniques

Zero-Based Budgeting

Zero-based budgeting requires starting from scratch for each new budgeting period, justifying every expense instead of merely adjusting previous budgets. This method forces business owners to evaluate each cost's necessity, promoting efficient resource allocation and control.

Incremental Budgeting

Incremental budgeting involves adjusting the previous budget's figures for the upcoming period. This method is less time-consuming but may overlook opportunities for cost reduction or efficiency improvements. It is useful when stable business conditions are expected, and past data provide a reliable basis for future projections.

Cash Flow Forecasting

Cash flow forecasting predicts cash inflows and outflows over a specific period. This tool is essential for maintaining liquidity, ensuring the business meets its obligations, and investing in growth opportunities. Regular forecasting helps identify potential cash shortfalls and allows for proactive management, such as adjusting credit terms or seeking additional financing.

Scenario Planning

Scenario planning involves preparing for future scenarios—best-case, worst-case, and most likely. This approach helps businesses anticipate changes in the market and their impacts on revenue and expenses. By considering different scenarios, business owners can develop contingency plans and remain agile in the face of uncertainty.

Securing Financing

Types of Financing Options Available

Traditional Loans

Traditional loans, such as bank loans, lines of credit, and Small Business Administration (SBA) loans, are standard financing options. These loans often have lower interest rates but require a strong credit history, collateral, and a detailed business plan. Lines of credit offer flexibility, allowing businesses to borrow up to a set limit and pay interest only on the amount used.

Alternative Financing

Alternative financing options, including peer-to-peer lending, crowdfunding, and micro-loans, have become increasingly popular. These options are often more accessible to businesses with limited credit history or collateral. Crowdfunding, in particular, allows businesses to raise small amounts of money from many people, often in exchange for early access to products or services.

Equity Financing

Equity financing involves raising capital by selling the business's shares to investors. This option can provide significant funding without the obligation to repay a loan, but it involves giving up a portion of ownership and control. Angel investors and venture capitalists are familiar equity financing sources, typically seeking high-growth potential businesses.

Preparing for Lender Meetings

Building a Strong Business Case

To secure financing, business owners must present a compelling business case to lenders or investors. This includes a detailed business plan, financial projections, and an explanation of how the funds will be used. Demonstrating an absolute understanding of the market, competitive landscape, and unique value proposition is crucial.

Understanding Lender Requirements

Lenders typically require a strong credit score, collateral, and favorable financial ratios, such as debt-to-equity and current ratios. Understanding these requirements helps business owners prepare for the application process and address potential concerns beforehand.

Negotiating Terms

Once approved for financing, negotiating favorable terms is essential. This includes interest rates, repayment schedules, and covenants—specific conditions the borrower must meet. It's essential to fully understand these terms and their implications for the business's cash flow and financial health.

Preparing Documentation

Having all necessary documentation ready is critical for a smooth application process. This includes financial statements, tax returns, legal documents, and relevant business licenses or permits. Proper preparation demonstrates professionalism and readiness to potential lenders or investors.

Cash Flow Analysis and Management Strategies

Monitoring Cash Inflows and Outflows

Effective cash flow management starts with closely monitoring cash inflows (sales, loans, investments) and outflows (expenses, debt payments, salaries). Regular tracking helps identify trends, such as seasonal fluctuations or changes in customer payment patterns, allowing for timely adjustments.

Cash Flow Optimization Techniques

Several strategies can optimize cash flow, such as speeding up receivables (offering discounts for early payments) and managing payables (negotiating longer payment terms with suppliers). Inventory management is also crucial—keeping inventory levels optimal prevents tying up too much cash in stock and reduces storage costs.

Building an Emergency Fund

Importance of a Cash Reserve

An emergency fund is a financial safety net, covering unexpected expenses like equipment repairs or economic downturns. It gives the business liquidity to navigate unforeseen challenges without using high-interest borrowing.

Setting Up an Emergency Fund

Business owners should determine an appropriate amount to establish an emergency fund based on their specific risk factors and industry standards. A reserve covering three to six months of operating expenses is recommended. Building this fund gradually and maintaining it is crucial for long-term financial stability.

Regular Financial Reviews and Performance Analysis

Monthly and Quarterly Reviews

Regular financial reviews, such as monthly and quarterly assessments, are essential for tracking progress against the budget and financial goals. These reviews provide an opportunity to evaluate performance, identify variances, and adjust strategies.

Key Financial Ratios

Financial ratios offer crucial insights into the business's financial health. Key ratios include liquidity ratios (current ratio, quick ratio), profitability ratios (gross profit margin, net profit margin), and leverage ratios (debt-to-equity ratio). Analyzing these ratios helps make informed investment, financing, and cost management decisions.

Identifying Financial Trends

Recognizing trends in revenue, expenses, and cash flow is vital for proactive financial management. These trends can indicate potential issues, such as declining sales or rising costs, allowing for early intervention and corrective actions.

Making Necessary Adjustments to the Financial Plan

Revising Budgets and Forecasts

Revising budgets and forecasts is crucial as the business environment evolves. This involves adjusting revenue projections, expense budgets, and cash flow forecasts based on actual performance and updated market data. Staying flexible and responsive helps maintain alignment with the business's strategic goals.

Implementing Cost-Saving Measures

Identifying areas for cost reduction is an ongoing process. This may include negotiating better rates with suppliers, optimizing operational processes, or reducing discretionary spending. Implementing these measures can free up resources for investment in growth initiatives.

Strategic Planning for Growth

Financial planning is not just about managing the present; it's also about preparing for the future. Strategic planning involves setting long-term financial goals, identifying expansion opportunities, and allocating resources for research and development, marketing, or new product lines. A well-thought-out growth strategy ensures the business continues to evolve and adapt to changing market conditions.

Financial planning and budgeting are critical to the success and sustainability of cash-based businesses. Business owners can create a solid financial foundation by understanding the critical components of a financial plan, implementing effective budgeting and forecasting techniques, securing the right financing, managing cash flow, and regularly reviewing financial performance. This foundation supports day-to-day operations and enables strategic growth and adaptation in a dynamic business environment. Prioritizing financial health and agility ensures the business can weather challenges and seize opportunities for long-term success.

CHAPTER 7

DESIGN AND CONSTRUCTION

The design and construction phase is pivotal in establishing a cash-based business, such as vending machines or car washes. This phase transforms your business idea into a tangible reality, setting the foundation for operational efficiency and customer satisfaction. The role of thoughtful design and robust construction cannot be overstated, as they are crucial in optimizing space utilization, ensuring compliance with regulations, and creating a positive customer experience. Whether strategically placing vending machines in high-traffic areas or designing a car wash to maximize vehicle throughput, the decisions made during this phase impact your business's success. This chapter will guide you through the planning, design, and construction processes, ensuring your business is built on a solid foundation ready to serve customers and drive profitability.

Part I: Planning Your Space

Understanding Your Requirements

The first step in planning your space is thoroughly understanding your business needs. For vending machine operators, this involves selecting locations with high foot traffic, good visibility, and easy accessibility. Consider the demographics of each location and the types of products that will appeal to potential customers. Planning for sufficient space around the machines for easy access and maintenance is also crucial.

The layout of car washes goes beyond the wash bays. To ensure a smooth traffic flow, you must consider areas for customer waiting, vacuuming stations, payment kiosks, and straightforward entry and exit points. Additionally, environmental considerations such as water drainage and recycling systems should be integrated into the design to comply with regulations and reduce operational costs.

Design Principles for Vending Machines and Car Washes

Vending machine design focuses on several fundamental principles: visibility, security, and accessibility. Machines should be placed in well-lit, easily visible areas to attract customers and deter vandalism. Accessibility is also crucial, ensuring all customers, including those with disabilities, can use the machines. Implementing security measures, such as surveillance cameras and durable machine construction, can protect against theft and vandalism.

Car washes require a design that prioritizes functionality and customer experience. Efficient vehicle flow from entry to exit is essential to minimize wait times and maximize the number of vehicles serviced. Considerations include the layout of wash bays, vacuuming areas, and payment systems. Incorporating environmentally friendly practices, such as water recycling systems, can enhance your business's appeal to eco-conscious customers and help comply with environmental regulations.

Engaging with Design Professionals

Hiring architects or design consultants specializing in retail and service industries can provide invaluable insights and ensure your space is optimized for functionality and customer experience. Communicating your vision clearly to these professionals is crucial. Share your business goals, target audience, and specific requirements or constraints. Detailed discussions during the design phase can prevent costly changes later on and ensure that the final design aligns with your business objectives.

Part II: Navigating the Construction Process

Securing the Correct Contractor

Choosing a construction contractor experienced in commercial projects similar to your business is vital. For vending machine installations, look for contractors who understand the technical requirements, including electrical work and securing machines. For car washes, find contractors experienced in building such facilities, as they require specialized knowledge in plumbing, electrical systems, and environmental compliance.

Conduct thorough due diligence by checking references, reviewing past projects, and ensuring the contractor has the necessary licenses and insurance. Visit completed projects to assess the quality of their work and talk to previous clients about their experience. This step helps ensure the contractor can deliver on time, within budget, and to the expected quality standards.

Understanding Construction Contracts

A clear, detailed construction contract is crucial for protecting your interests. The contract should outline the scope of work, timelines, budget, payment schedules, and quality standards. Key terms include clauses on change orders, which specify how changes to the project scope will be handled, and warranties on materials and quality.

Negotiating favorable contract terms can prevent misunderstandings and protect you from unexpected costs. Ensure the contract includes provisions for dealing with delays and cost overruns, specifying penalties for late completion, and procedures for resolving disputes. Consulting with a legal professional to review the contract can help protect your rights.

Construction Phase: Oversight and Management

Effective oversight is crucial during construction to ensure adherence to plans, timelines, and budgets. Regular site visits are essential to monitor progress and address issues promptly. Employing a project manager can be beneficial; they act as your representative on-site, coordinating between you and the contractor, ensuring that work progresses smoothly, and keeping the project on track.

Clear communication with your contractor and project manager is vital. Set up regular meetings to review progress, discuss issues, and make necessary adjustments. This proactive approach can prevent minor problems from becoming significant delays or cost overruns.

Dealing with Delays and Overruns

Construction delays and cost overruns, often caused by unexpected weather conditions, supply chain disruptions, or specifications or design changes, are common challenges. To effectively manage these, having a robust contingency plan is a must. This plan should include setting aside a contingency budget to cover unexpected expenses and being flexible with timelines.

When managing potential delays, clear communication with your contractor is critical. Understanding the root causes of these delays is not just important but crucial. It empowers you to make informed decisions, such as adjusting the project scope or seeking alternative solutions, to keep the project on track. Regular updates and transparency from your contractor are essential to manage expectations and minimize disruptions.

Part III: Preparing for Launch

Installation and Testing of Equipment

Once construction is complete, the next step is installing and testing equipment. This includes ensuring vending machines are correctly placed, stocked, and functional. Car washes involve installing washing and drying equipment, payment systems, and additional features like vacuum stations or detailing bays.

Testing is crucial to ensure all equipment operates correctly and meets safety standards. This includes running through the customer experience to ensure that machines are easy to use, payments are processed smoothly, and, for car washes, that vehicles are cleaned efficiently and effectively. Any issues identified during testing should be addressed promptly to ensure a smooth launch.

Final Inspections and Compliance Checks

Before opening, final inspections and necessary approvals and certifications from local authorities must be conducted. This ensures your business complies with all relevant health, safety, and environmental regulations. For car washes, this may include water usage and disposal compliance checks. For vending machines, ensure that all products are stored and displayed according to health and safety standards.

Completing these inspections and obtaining the necessary documentation ensures legal compliance and peace of mind that your business is safe and ready to operate.

Training Staff and Preparing for Operations

Training your staff is the final step in preparing for launch. They should be well-versed in operating all equipment, providing excellent customer service, and handling issues. For vending machines, this includes training on restocking, maintenance, and handling customer inquiries. For car washes, staff should be trained to use washing equipment, manage traffic flow, and address customer concerns.

Final preparations include stockpiling inventory, setting up marketing campaigns, and finalizing operational procedures. These ensure a smooth opening and position your business for immediate success.

The path from concept to reality involves careful planning, strategic decision-making, and effective execution. From understanding your space requirements to designing a customer-friendly layout and navigating the construction process, each step lays the foundation for your business's future success. The construction phase is not without its challenges, but with the right team and proactive management, these challenges can be overcome.

As you transition from construction to operations, the excitement of bringing your vision to life culminates in the launch of your business. This chapter provided the roadmap to ensure your design and construction efforts succeed, setting the stage for a thriving business. By following these guidelines, you can confidently navigate the complexities of building your business, turning your vision into a reality that attracts customers and drives profitability.

CHAPTER 8

PURCHASING EQUIPMENT AND SUPPLIES

The Essentials of Operations

Your choice of equipment and supplies is a critical factor in the success of your cash-based business, whether vending machines, car washes, or laundromats. The quality and reliability of your equipment directly impact your service efficiency, customer satisfaction, and overall profitability. This chapter explores the critical considerations for selecting and acquiring the necessary equipment and supplies, including identifying specific needs, sourcing suppliers, understanding financing and leasing options, and planning ongoing maintenance.

Identifying Equipment Needs

Vending Machines

Types of Vending Machines

The first step in identifying equipment needs is understanding the different types of vending machines available and choosing the ones that best suit your business model and target market. Common types include snack machines, beverage machines, combo machines (offering snacks and drinks), and specialty machines (dispensing fresh food or electronics). The choice depends on location, target audience, and the products you plan to offer.

Assessing Location and Demographics

The location of your vending machines significantly influences the type of equipment you need. High-traffic areas like shopping malls or office buildings may benefit from machines offering various products. At the same time, specialized locations like gyms or schools might require machines with healthy snacks or educational supplies. Understanding the demographics of your target market helps tailor your offerings to meet specific preferences and needs.

Features and Specifications

Modern vending machines have various features, including cashless payment systems, energy efficiency, remote monitoring, and advanced security features. Cashless systems, such as credit/debit card readers and mobile payment options, cater to the increasing preference for cashless transactions. Remote monitoring technology allows operators to track inventory levels and sales in real-time, optimizing restocking schedules and reducing operational costs.

Car Washes

Types of Car Wash Systems

Car wash businesses can choose from various systems, including self-service bays, automated tunnel washes, and in-bay automatic systems. Each system has different requirements and benefits:

- **Self-Service Bays**: These systems allow customers to wash their cars using provided equipment. They are cost-effective but require more space and customer involvement.

- **Automated Tunnel Washes**: Use conveyor belts to move cars through cleaning stages. They provide high throughput and a consistent wash quality but require significant upfront investment.

- **In-Bay Automatic Systems**: Vehicles remain stationary while automated equipment moves around them. These systems are space-efficient and suitable for locations with limited space.

Determining Service Offerings

The equipment and chemicals needed will depend on the services you plan to offer, such as basic washes, waxing, detailing, or eco-friendly options. Offering various services can attract a broader customer base and increase revenue opportunities.

Considerations for Location and Traffic

The location and expected traffic volume will influence the type of car wash system you choose. High-traffic areas may justify the investment in automated systems to handle large volumes efficiently, while lower-traffic areas might benefit from self-service or in-bay systems.

Laundromats

Types of Laundry Equipment

Laundromat equipment includes washers, dryers, folding tables, and ancillary equipment like change machines and detergent dispensers. Key considerations include:

- **Washers and Dryers**: Commercial-grade machines are essential for durability and efficiency. Consider the capacity, energy efficiency, and specific features like programmable cycles and moisture sensors.

- **Ancillary Equipment**: Items like folding tables, laundry carts, and vending machines for detergent and other laundry supplies enhance the customer experience.

Determining Capacity and Volume

Assess the expected customer volume and peak usage times to determine the number and type of machines needed. Larger capacity machines can handle bulkier items and reduce customer wait times, enhancing customer satisfaction.

Service Offerings and Customer Amenities

Additional services such as wash-and-fold, dry cleaning, and pick-up/drop-off services can differentiate your business and provide additional revenue streams. Customer amenities like free Wi-Fi, comfortable seating, and child-friendly areas can also enhance the customer experience and encourage repeat business.

Sourcing Suppliers and Vendors

Finding Reliable Suppliers

Research and Recommendations

Research potential suppliers and vendors through industry associations, trade shows, and online reviews. Networking with other business owners and industry professionals can provide valuable recommendations and insights into dependable suppliers.

Evaluating Supplier Reliability

Consider factors such as the supplier's reputation, years in business, and customer service. A reliable supplier should offer high-quality products, timely delivery, and responsive support. Checking references and speaking with other customers can help gauge the supplier's reliability and customer service quality.

Comparing Prices and Warranties

Obtaining quotes from multiple suppliers allows for the comparison of prices and terms. Beyond the initial cost, consider the long-term value, including warranties, maintenance services, and the availability of replacement parts. A slightly higher upfront cost may be justified if it includes a comprehensive warranty and vital support services.

Negotiating Contracts and Warranties

Contract Negotiation

Negotiating terms with suppliers is a critical step in securing favorable conditions. Key negotiation points include pricing, payment terms, delivery schedules, and delay penalties. Ensure that the contract clearly outlines all terms and conditions, including the responsibilities of both parties.

Understanding Warranties

Warranties are crucial for protecting your investment in equipment. Ensure that the warranty covers parts, labor, and service. Understand the warranty claim process and any applicable limitations or exclusions. A robust warranty can provide peace of mind and reduce unexpected repair costs down the road.

Service Agreements

Consider establishing a service agreement with the supplier, especially for complex equipment like car wash systems. Service agreements often include regular maintenance, emergency repairs, and technical support, ensuring that equipment remains operational and efficient.

Financing and Leasing Options

Comparison of Purchasing vs. Leasing Equipment

Purchasing Equipment

Purchasing equipment outright requires a significant upfront investment but provides complete ownership and control. Benefits include potential tax deductions for depreciation and the absence of ongoing lease payments. However, it also ties up capital that could be used for other business needs.

Leasing Equipment

Leasing equipment is a strategic move for businesses with limited capital, as it provides access to the latest technology with lower upfront costs. The lease payments are typically considered operating expenses, offering potential tax benefits. However, it's important to note that leasing does not build equity, and the total cost over time may be higher than purchasing.

Deciding Factors

The decision between purchasing and leasing depends on factors like cash flow, capital availability, and the equipment's expected lifespan. Businesses prioritizing cash flow flexibility and access to the latest technology may prefer leasing, while those focused on long-term ownership and equity building may opt for purchasing.

Exploring Financing Options

Traditional Bank Loans

Traditional bank loans offer a lump sum of capital, repaid over time with interest. They require a strong credit history and collateral but typically offer lower interest rates than other financing options.

Equipment Financing

Equipment financing is specifically designed to purchase equipment. The equipment itself often serves as collateral, which can make it easier to qualify for financing. This option allows businesses to acquire necessary equipment without a significant upfront investment.

Leasing Companies and Vendors

Some equipment suppliers and leasing companies offer in-house financing options. These convenient arrangements may include flexible terms, such as seasonal payment plans. However, comparing these options with external financing is essential to ensure competitive rates and terms.

Maintenance Considerations

Planning for Equipment Maintenance and Replacement

Routine Maintenance

Regular maintenance is essential for ensuring equipment longevity and reliability. This includes scheduled inspections, cleaning, and servicing. Establishing a maintenance schedule helps prevent breakdowns and costly repairs, keeping operations smooth and uninterrupted.

Predictive Maintenance

Predictive maintenance techniques, such as monitoring performance data and conducting regular diagnostic tests, can identify potential issues before they become serious problems. This proactive approach can minimize downtime and extend the life of the equipment.

Replacement Planning

Equipment has a finite lifespan, and planning for eventual replacement is crucial. By monitoring the condition and performance of equipment regularly and setting aside funds for replacement as needed, you can be proactive and in control, ensuring that unexpected equipment failures do not disrupt business operations.

Setting Up Maintenance Schedules

Creating a Maintenance Calendar

A crucial step is developing a detailed maintenance calendar that includes all routine and preventive maintenance tasks. This calendar should specify the frequency of each task, such as daily cleaning, weekly inspections, and annual servicing. Keeping a log of completed maintenance helps track the equipment's condition and ensures accountability.

Training Staff on Maintenance Procedures

Proper training ensures that staff can perform basic maintenance tasks and recognize signs of potential problems. This training should cover daily upkeep, such as cleaning, checking for apparent issues, and reporting procedures for more complex problems requiring professional attention.

Outsourcing Maintenance and Repairs

For more complex equipment, consider outsourcing maintenance and repairs to professionals. Establish relationships with reliable service providers familiar with your equipment and can offer timely support. Outsourcing ensures that maintenance is performed correctly and efficiently, minimizing the risk of operational disruptions.

Investing in the Right Equipment and Supplies

Investing in the right equipment and supplies is critical to establishing and maintaining a successful cash-based business. Whether you operate vending machines, car washes, or laundromats, choosing the appropriate equipment, sourcing reliable suppliers, securing favorable financing, and planning maintenance are all essential. By carefully considering these factors, business owners can ensure that their operations are efficient, reliable, and capable of delivering high-quality customer service. Proper investment in equipment and supplies supports day-to-day operations and contributes to long-term business growth and profitability.

CHAPTER 9

SETTING UP FOR OPERATIONS

Introduction: The Final Steps Before Launch

The setup phase culminates in planning and preparation, where your business concept becomes a reality. For cash-based enterprises like vending machines, car washes, and laundromats, a seamless operational setup is not just about getting the equipment up and running; it's about creating an environment that meets customer needs and supports efficient, ongoing operations. This chapter will walk you through the essential steps to ensure your business is operationally sound and customer-ready.

Installation and Initial Setup

Vending Machines

Installing vending machines involves securing them in high-traffic areas, ensuring they are adequately powered, and filling them with a selection of products tailored to the target audience. Early decisions on cash-based or digital payment options will affect the initial setup and the day-to-day management.

Car Washes

For car washes, the setup includes installing wash equipment, payment systems, and necessary environmental systems like water recycling. The layout should facilitate a smooth flow of vehicles, with clear signage to guide customers through the process.

Laundromats

Setting up a laundromat requires installing commercial-grade washers and dryers, ensuring robust utility connections, and providing customers easy access to laundry products through vending machines or a service counter.

Operational Systems and Processes

Creating efficient operational workflows is crucial across all three business types. Implementing inventory tracking systems helps manage stock levels and predict reorder times, while financial accounting systems keep track of revenues and expenses. Customer service protocols ensure that staff can effectively address customer needs and maintain high satisfaction levels.

Staffing and Training

Although vending machines might require minimal staffing, regular restocking and maintenance are crucial. Car washes and laundromats benefit significantly from well-trained staff who can enhance the customer experience through excellent service and maintain operational efficiency.

Preparing for Soft Launch and Grand Opening

A soft launch allows you to fine-tune operations with a limited audience, while a grand opening is your opportunity to introduce your business to the wider community. Effective marketing and promotional strategies can attract an initial customer base and build momentum for sustained business growth.

CHAPTER 10

MARKETING AND CUSTOMER ENGAGEMENT

Building Your Brand

This structured approach to Chapter 10 provides a foundation for detailing the operational setup process for vending machines, car washes, and laundromats. Expanding on each section will ensure comprehensive guidance for entrepreneurs, from equipment installation to successfully launching their businesses.

Marketing and customer engagement are not just tasks but crucial strategies for cash-based businesses like vending machines and car washes. Effective marketing attracts new customers and helps retain existing ones, while solid customer engagement fosters loyalty and word-of-mouth promotion. This chapter explores strategies for building your brand, promoting your services, and connecting with customers to enhance their experience. Understanding your target market and leveraging various marketing tools and techniques can create a compelling brand presence and cultivate lasting customer relationships. This chapter will guide you through developing a marketing plan, utilizing digital and traditional marketing methods, and implementing customer engagement strategies to drive business growth and profitability.

Part I: Developing a Marketing Plan

Identifying Your Target Market

The first step in developing a marketing plan is identifying your target market. For vending machines, this might include office workers, students, or shoppers in high-traffic areas. For car washes, the target audience could range from busy professionals seeking quick, convenient services to car enthusiasts interested in premium detailing.

Conducting market research helps you understand the demographics, preferences, and behaviors of your target customers. Surveys, focus groups, and analysis of competitor offerings can provide valuable insights. Understanding your target market allows you to tailor your marketing messages and services to meet their needs and preferences.

Setting Marketing Objectives

Clear, measurable marketing objectives are essential for guiding your marketing efforts. Objectives may include increasing brand awareness, driving traffic to specific locations, or boosting sales of certain products or services. Setting realistic and achievable goals provides a benchmark for evaluating the effectiveness of your marketing strategies and helps you allocate resources efficiently.

Budgeting and Resource Allocation

Determining your marketing budget involves assessing the costs associated with various marketing activities, such as advertising, promotions, and digital marketing. Allocating resources effectively ensures that you can execute your marketing plan without overspending. Consider each marketing channel's return on investment (ROI) to prioritize spending on the most effective strategies.

Part II: Utilizing Digital and Traditional Marketing

Digital Marketing Strategies

Digital marketing is a powerful tool for reaching a broad audience and engaging customers. Key digital marketing strategies include:

1. **Social Media Marketing:** Platforms like Facebook, Instagram, and Twitter allow you to reach your target audience, promote your services, and engage with customers in real-time. Sharing content, running promotions, and responding to customer inquiries can enhance brand visibility and engagement.

2. **Search Engine Optimization (SEO):** Optimizing your website for search engines helps improve its visibility in search results, attracting more potential customers to your site. To enhance your SEO efforts, focus on relevant keywords, high-quality content, and a user-friendly website design.

3. **Email Marketing:** Building an email list allows you to communicate directly with customers, sharing news, promotions, and updates. Personalized email campaigns can help build relationships and encourage repeat business.

4. **Online Advertising:** Pay-per-click (PPC) advertising and social media ads can target specific demographics, driving traffic to your website or physical locations. Setting a clear objective and monitoring performance metrics are crucial for maximizing the ROI of online ads.

Traditional Marketing Techniques

While digital marketing is essential, traditional marketing techniques also play a vital role in reaching customers:

1. **Print Advertising:** Local newspapers, magazines, and flyers can effectively reach a local audience. Highlighting special offers, new services, or unique selling points can attract new customers.

2. **Outdoor Advertising:** Billboards, banners, and signage in high-traffic areas can increase brand visibility. For car washes, clear signage directing traffic to your location is crucial.

3. **Direct Mail:** Sending promotional materials or coupons directly to potential customers' homes can be a targeted way to drive traffic and sales.

4. **Events and Sponsorships:** Participating in local events or sponsoring community activities can increase brand awareness and build positive associations with your business.

Part III: Customer Engagement Strategies

Enhancing the Customer Experience

Creating a positive customer experience is critical to building loyalty and encouraging repeat business. For vending machines, this means ensuring machines are always stocked, clean, and easy to use. Offering a variety of products, including healthy and specialty items, can cater to diverse customer preferences. For car washes, providing excellent service, maintaining clean and comfortable facilities, and offering additional services like detailing or interior cleaning can enhance the overall experience.

Loyalty Programs and Promotions

Loyalty programs are an effective way to incentivize repeat business and reward loyal customers. Consider offering a points-based system where customers earn rewards for frequent purchases or visits. For example, a car wash could offer a free wash after a certain number of visits. Additionally, seasonal promotions or special discounts can attract new customers and encourage existing customers to use your services.

Engaging with Customers Online

Active engagement with customers on social media and other online platforms helps build a strong brand presence and fosters a sense of community. Responding promptly to comments and inquiries, sharing user-generated content, and running online contests or giveaways can increase customer interaction and loyalty. Encouraging customers to leave reviews and testimonials enhancing your business's credibility and attracts new customers.

Building and Sustaining a Strong Brand

Effective marketing and customer engagement are essential for the success and growth of cash-based businesses like vending machines and car washes. By developing a comprehensive marketing plan, utilizing both digital and traditional marketing methods, and implementing customer engagement strategies, you can build a strong brand and cultivate lasting customer relationships. Understanding your target market, setting clear objectives, and allocating resources efficiently is vital to executing a successful marketing strategy. Engaging with online and offline customers enhances their experience and fosters loyalty, driving repeat business and word-of-mouth referrals. As you continue to grow your business, focusing on customer satisfaction and adapting your marketing strategies to changing market trends will ensure long-term success and profitability.

Part III
Growth and Sustainability

CHAPTER 11

MARKETING AND GRAND OPENING

The Power of Effective Marketing

Effective marketing is crucial for success in the competitive landscape of cash-based businesses such as vending machines, car washes, and laundromats. It's not just about visibility; it's about reaching the right audience with a compelling message at the right time. A strategic marketing plan and a well-executed grand opening can significantly influence your business's initial and long-term success. This chapter provides comprehensive strategies for building a solid brand, engaging potential customers, and launching your business with a memorable impact. By understanding the fundamentals of marketing and the importance of a grand opening, you can set the stage for sustained growth and profitability.

Building Your Marketing Plan

Market Analysis

Understanding your target audience and the competitive landscape is the first step in crafting an effective marketing plan. For vending machines, this might mean identifying locations with high foot traffic, such as schools, offices, or shopping centers, and understanding the demographic characteristics of those areas. The focus for car washes and laundromats might be on residential neighborhoods or areas with limited access to similar services. Market research helps identify potential customers' needs and preferences, allowing you to tailor your offerings and marketing messages accordingly.

Branding

Developing a unique brand identity is crucial for differentiating your business from competitors. This includes creating a memorable logo, choosing a color scheme, and crafting a consistent brand message that resonates with your target market. Your brand should reflect your business's core values and benefits, whether convenience, quality, or reliability. For example, a car wash might emphasize eco-friendly practices, while a vending machine service could highlight the variety and freshness of its snacks.

Marketing Channels

Choosing the right mix of marketing channels is essential for reaching your target audience. Online channels such as social media and email marketing can effectively reach a broad audience and engage with them directly. Print advertising, including flyers and local newspaper ads, can also help reach local customers. Outdoor advertising, such as banners and signage, can increase visibility and draw attention to your business location. Additionally, partnerships with local businesses and community events can enhance your brand's presence and reach.

Digital Marketing Strategies

Website and SEO

A well-designed, user-friendly website is a central hub for your digital marketing efforts. It should provide transparent information about your services, locations, pricing, and promotions. Optimizing your website for search engines (SEO) is crucial to improving your visibility in local search results. This involves using relevant keywords, creating high-quality content, and ensuring your website is mobile-friendly. A strong SEO strategy can help attract potential customers searching for services like yours.

Social Media

Social media platforms such as Instagram, Facebook, and Twitter are powerful tools for engaging with the community and showcasing your business. Regularly posting updates, promotions, and customer testimonials can help build a loyal following. For example, you can share before-and-after photos of car washes, highlight new vending machine products, or showcase the cleanliness and amenities of your laundromat. Engaging with followers through comments and messages fosters a sense of community and customer loyalty.

Email Marketing

Building a subscriber list lets you communicate directly with customers about promotions, new services, or special events. Personalized email campaigns can nurture customer relationships and encourage repeat business. For example, sending out a monthly newsletter with tips on car maintenance, laundry care, or healthy snack options can provide value to your customers and keep your business in mind.

Traditional Marketing and Community Engagement

Flyers and Local Ads

Despite the digital age, traditional marketing methods like flyers and local ads remain compelling, especially for local businesses. You can attract your business by distributing eye-catching flyers in nearby neighborhoods, shopping centers, and other high-traffic areas. Investing in ads in local newspapers or community bulletin boards can also help reach residents who prefer traditional media.

Partnerships and Sponsorships

Collaborating with local businesses, schools, and community organizations can enhance visibility and credibility. For instance, partnering with a local cafe to place vending machines or sponsoring a local sports team can provide mutual benefits and increase exposure. Sponsorship opportunities at community events, such as fairs or charity runs, can also provide a platform for direct interaction with potential customers.

Word of Mouth

One of the most effective marketing strategies is encouraging satisfied customers to spread the word about your business. Word-of-mouth recommendations are highly trusted and can significantly influence potential customers. Offering incentives, such as discounts or free referral services, can motivate customers to recommend your business to friends and family.

Planning Your Grand Opening

Soft Launch vs. Grand Opening

A soft launch involves opening your business to a limited audience before the official grand opening. This approach allows you to test operations, identify and fix issues, and refine your services. A grand opening, on the other hand, is a public event aimed at attracting many potential customers and generating buzz. Whether to have a soft launch, a grand opening, or both depends on your readiness and marketing goals.

Event Planning

Planning a grand opening event involves more than just opening your doors. Consider offering special promotions, discounts, or giveaways to attract customers. Live entertainment, such as music or performances, can create a festive atmosphere. Providing free samples or demonstrations can also encourage visitors to try your services. For example, a car wash could offer free car washes for the first 50 customers, or a laundromat could provide complimentary wash-and-fold services.

Promotion

Promoting your grand opening is crucial for ensuring a high turnout. Use a mix of marketing channels, including social media, local media, and community outreach, to spread the word.

Create event pages on social media platforms and encourage attendees to RSVP and share the event with their networks. Engaging local bloggers and influencers to cover the event can amplify your reach. Ensure that all promotional materials highlight the unique aspects of your business and the benefits of attending the grand opening.

Case Study: A Launch to Remember

Consider the case of "Quick Clean," a new laundromat that planned a memorable grand opening. Quick Clean used a combination of digital and traditional marketing strategies to promote their event. They created a vibrant social media campaign showcasing their modern facilities and unique services, such as eco-friendly detergent options and a comfortable waiting area with free Wi-Fi. They also partnered with a local cafe to provide free coffee and snacks during the event.

On the day of the grand opening, Quick Clean offered special promotions, including free laundry services for the first 100 customers and discounted rates for the first month. They also hosted a live DJ to entertain attendees and create a lively atmosphere. The event attracted a large crowd, resulting in a strong customer turnout and positive word-of-mouth. The grand opening's success set the stage for Quick Clean's long-term success, demonstrating the impact of thoughtful planning and effective marketing.

Setting the Stage for Long-Term Success

A solid marketing strategy and a well-executed grand opening are foundational to establishing and growing a successful cash-based business. You can effectively reach and engage your target audience by thoroughly understanding your market, building a solid brand identity, and leveraging a mix of digital and traditional marketing channels. The grand opening event provides an opportunity to make a memorable first impression and attract a loyal customer base.

Continued marketing efforts are essential for maintaining momentum and adapting to changing market trends. Regularly evaluating and refining your strategies based on customer feedback and performance metrics will help sustain your business's growth and success. By prioritizing customer engagement and maintaining a strong brand presence, you can set the stage for long-term profitability and business growth.

CHAPTER 12

DAILY OPERATIONS MANAGEMENT

The Backbone of Your Business

Daily operations management is the backbone of any business, particularly for cash-based operations like vending machines, car washes, and laundromats. It involves meticulously coordinating various tasks to ensure smooth functioning, high efficiency, and customer satisfaction. Effective daily management is not just about maintaining operations; it's about optimizing every aspect of your business to maximize profitability and enhance the customer experience. This chapter provides actionable strategies for streamlining operations, leveraging technology, managing finances, and fostering a positive work environment. By focusing on these areas, you can build a strong foundation for long-term success and competitiveness in the market.

Streamlining Operations for Efficiency

Vending Machines

Efficient management of vending machines starts with robust inventory management. Regular monitoring of stock levels is essential to ensure machines are always well-stocked, meeting customer demand without overstocking, which can lead to waste. Implementing a schedule for restocking based on data-driven insights helps optimize routes and reduce fuel costs. Routine maintenance is crucial to prevent downtime; this includes cleaning machines, checking payment systems, and ensuring the machines are fully functional. Additionally, remote monitoring technology can provide real-time inventory levels and machine status updates, allowing for proactive management.

Car Washes

Operational efficiency hinges on effective scheduling and equipment maintenance for car washes. Scheduling services to minimize customer wait times is critical, as long waits can lead to dissatisfaction. Implementing an appointment system or queue management can streamline the flow of vehicles. Regular maintenance of wash equipment, including cleaning nozzles and replacing worn-out brushes, ensures consistent service quality. Water reclamation systems can significantly reduce water consumption and operational costs, aligning with environmental regulations and appealing to eco-conscious customers.

Laundromats

In laundromats, the focus should be on machine maintenance and facility cleanliness. Regularly servicing washing machines and dryers prevents breakdowns and prolongs equipment life. Ensuring the facility is clean and welcoming is crucial for attracting and retaining customers. This includes maintaining the cleanliness of floors, folding areas, and restrooms. Additionally, offering additional services, such as Wi-Fi, coffee vending, or detergent sales, can enhance the customer experience and generate additional revenue. Monitoring usage patterns can help optimize the placement and mix of machines, ensuring that popular machines are readily available during peak times.

Enhancing Customer Experience

All Businesses

In today's competitive market, customer experience is a key differentiator. Integrating technology into your operations can significantly enhance convenience and satisfaction. For instance, implementing mobile payment options in vending machines and laundromats can streamline transactions and appeal to tech-savvy customers. Car washes can benefit from automated payment systems and loyalty programs that reward frequent visitors, encouraging repeat business.

Creating a pleasant environment is equally important. This means clean and well-maintained units in secure, well-lit areas for vending machines. Providing comfortable, safe waiting areas with amenities like free Wi-Fi or refreshments in car washes can improve the customer experience. Laundromats should offer a clean, safe, and comfortable space, possibly with entertainment options like TVs or magazines.

Customer feedback mechanisms, such as suggestion boxes or online reviews, are valuable for gauging customer satisfaction and identifying areas for improvement. Responding to feedback promptly and positively can enhance your reputation and customer loyalty. Consistently delivering a high-quality experience encourages positive word-of-mouth and builds a loyal customer base.

Financial Management and Optimization

Regular financial reviews are essential for assessing the health of your business. This involves tracking revenue, managing costs, and analyzing profitability. Keeping a close eye on financial metrics helps identify trends and areas for improvement, such as adjusting pricing based on demand or seasonal variations. This could mean adjusting product prices or introducing premium options for vending machines. Offering bundled services or subscription models in car washes can provide stable revenue streams. For laundromats, optimizing machine usage rates and exploring additional revenue opportunities, such as selling laundry products, can enhance profitability.

Cost management is another critical aspect. This includes negotiating with suppliers for better rates, managing utility costs, and ensuring operational expenses are kept in check. Exploring new revenue streams, such as offering advertising space on vending machines or car wash facilities, can also contribute to overall profitability.

Managing Staff and Operations

Hiring, training, and retaining quality employees is crucial for the smooth operation of your business. When hiring, look for individuals who align with your business values and have the skills to perform their roles effectively. Training should cover not only the technical aspects of the job but also customer service skills. Well-trained employees are better equipped to handle customer interactions, troubleshoot issues, and maintain equipment.

Retaining employees involves creating a positive work environment and offering competitive compensation and benefits. Recognition and career development opportunities can also contribute to employee satisfaction and retention. Leadership is critical to fostering a supportive workplace culture where employees feel valued and motivated.

Regular staff meetings and clear communication channels ensure everyone is aligned with the business goals and operational procedures. This helps maintain consistent service quality and address any operational challenges promptly. In businesses like car washes and laundromats, where customer service is a direct touchpoint, having a friendly and knowledgeable staff can significantly enhance the customer experience and contribute to the business's success.

Case Study: Clean & Shine Car Wash

> Clean & Shine Car Wash exemplifies operational excellence. By implementing a *streamlined scheduling system, they minimized customer wait*

times and maximized throughput. They introduced a membership program that provided unlimited washes for a fixed monthly fee, ensuring steady revenue and customer loyalty. Additionally, they invested in eco-friendly technologies like water reclamation systems, significantly reducing water consumption and operational costs.

To enhance customer experience, Clean & Shine offered amenities like a comfortable waiting area with refreshments and a children's play zone. They also installed a digital feedback system, allowing customers to rate their service and provide comments. This feedback was reviewed regularly, leading to continuous service improvements.

The staff at Clean & Shine was well-trained, not only in operating the equipment but also in customer service. This comprehensive training ensured that customers received a consistent, high-quality experience. The company's leadership emphasized a positive work culture, which helped retain skilled employees and maintain high service standards.

Clean & Shine's attention to operational detail, customer experience, and environmental responsibility set them apart in the market. Their success story demonstrates the impact of effective daily operations management on customer satisfaction and business profitability.

Operational Excellence as Your Competitive Edge

Operational excellence is not just about keeping your business running smoothly; it's about creating a competitive edge in the market. By focusing on efficient operations, enhancing the customer experience, and sound financial management, you can build a robust foundation for your business. Regularly assessing and adapting your operations ensures you meet evolving customer expectations and market demands. As demonstrated by the success stories in this chapter, businesses prioritizing operational efficiency and customer satisfaction are better positioned for long-term growth and success. Embracing a continuous improvement mindset and fostering a positive workplace culture will keep your business ahead of the competition, ensuring that your operations remain a key driver of your success.

CHAPTER 13

MAINTENANCE AND UPKEEP

The Importance of Regular Maintenance

Maintenance and upkeep are vital to the longevity and success of any cash-based business, including vending machines, car washes, and laundromats. Regular maintenance ensures equipment operates efficiently, minimizing downtime and preventing costly repairs. It also helps maintain a clean and welcoming environment, crucial for customer satisfaction and retention. This chapter aims to provide business owners with comprehensive strategies for establishing a routine maintenance schedule, implementing preventive measures, and managing repairs effectively. By prioritizing maintenance, businesses can protect their investments, enhance operational efficiency, and offer a consistently positive customer experience.

Creating a Maintenance Schedule

Vending Machines

A regular maintenance schedule is essential for vending machines to ensure operational efficiency and customer satisfaction. Routine inspections should include checking for mechanical issues, such as faulty payment systems or jammed dispensers. Cleaning is also critical to prevent product contamination and maintain an appealing appearance. Establishing a restocking schedule based on sales data helps keep popular items available while also providing an opportunity to inspect and clean the machines. Monitoring temperature controls, especially for machines dispensing perishable items, ensures product quality.

Car Washes

Car washes require a comprehensive maintenance schedule to maintain equipment performance and safety. Regular checks should include inspecting wash equipment for wear and tear, such as nozzle blockages or conveyor belt issues. Assessing the chemical balance of cleaning agents ensures optimal cleaning results and protects the vehicle surfaces. Additionally, a cleaning routine for the facility, including the wash bays and vacuum areas, helps create a positive customer experience. Implementing water reclamation systems can also reduce costs and environmental impact, making it a crucial part of the maintenance routine.

Laundromats

Daily cleaning and periodic maintenance are essential in laundromats to prevent equipment failures and ensure a pleasant customer environment. Regular maintenance checks should cover washers and dryers, focusing on issues like clogged filters, drum alignment, and belt wear. Vent cleaning is essential to prevent lint buildup, which can pose a fire hazard. A schedule for inspecting and cleaning detergent dispensers and lint traps can prevent malfunctions and extend the life of the machines. Keeping the facility clean, including floors and restrooms, is crucial for customer satisfaction.

Preventive Maintenance Strategies

Preventive maintenance is a proactive approach to managing equipment and facility upkeep. It involves regular inspections and servicing to identify and address minor issues before they escalate into major problems. For vending machines, this might include routine checks of electrical components and updating software systems to ensure security and efficiency. In car washes, preventive maintenance can involve regularly replacing worn-out brushes or checking water pressure systems to prevent equipment damage.

Preventive maintenance can reduce unexpected downtime, extend the lifespan of equipment, and minimize repair costs. Developing a preventive maintenance plan tailored to your business involves setting a schedule for inspections and servicing, keeping detailed records of maintenance activities, and training staff to recognize potential issues. By implementing these strategies, businesses can maintain a high standard of service and reliability.

Handling Repairs: DIY vs. Professional Services

Deciding whether to handle repairs in-house or hire professional services depends on the complexity of the issue and the expertise required. Simple repairs, such as replacing a broken vending machine light or unclogging a washing machine drain, can often be handled by trained staff. However, more complex issues like electrical faults or significant mechanical failures may require professional intervention.

Building a network of reliable service providers is crucial for handling specialized repairs. A list of contacts for electricians, plumbers, and equipment specialists can expedite the repair process and minimize downtime. Establishing a relationship with these professionals is also essential, as well as ensuring they understand your business needs and can provide timely and cost-effective solutions. While DIY repairs can save money, professional services are often necessary for complex problems, ensuring repairs are done correctly and safely.

Facility Upkeep and Cleanliness

Maintaining a clean and well-kept facility is critical for creating a positive customer experience. For vending machines, this means ensuring the surrounding area is free from litter and debris, which can deter customers. Regularly cleaning the machines, including the exterior and dispensing areas, is also crucial for hygiene and aesthetics.

Facility upkeep in car washes involves keeping wash bays, vacuuming, and waiting areas clean and orderly. This includes removing trash, cleaning windows, and ensuring the premises are free from water puddles and slippery surfaces. For laundromats, cleanliness extends to the machines, folding areas, and restrooms. Regular sweeping, mopping, and sanitizing surfaces help maintain a welcoming environment. Hiring professional cleaning services for deep cleaning can ensure high standards are maintained, particularly in areas that require specialized cleaning techniques.

Case Study: Spotless Clean Laundromat exemplifies excellence in maintenance and upkeep. The owners implemented a rigorous maintenance schedule, including daily cleaning of machines and facilities and weekly deep cleaning sessions. They also conducted monthly inspections of all equipment, checking for signs of wear and potential issues. This proactive approach allowed them to address minor problems before they became significant repairs, significantly reducing downtime.

Spotless Clean also invested in preventive maintenance training for their staff, enabling them to perform basic repairs and maintenance tasks. They established strong relationships with local service providers, ensuring quick response times for more complex issues. The laundromat's commitment to cleanliness and operational efficiency resulted in high customer satisfaction and repeat business. Customers appreciated the consistently clean environment and the reliability of the machines, which were always in good working order.

This case study highlights the importance of a well-planned maintenance strategy and its impact on customer satisfaction and business success. Spotless Clean's dedication to maintenance enhanced its reputation and contributed to long-term cost savings and operational efficiency.

Maintenance as a Pillar of Success

Maintenance and upkeep are critical components of running a successful cash-based business. Regular maintenance extends the life of equipment, reduces operational costs, and enhances the customer experience. Business owners can ensure their operations run smoothly and efficiently by implementing a structured maintenance schedule, investing in preventive maintenance, and knowing when to call in professionals. Clean and well-maintained facilities attract and retain customers, creating a positive impression and encouraging repeat business. Embracing maintenance as a core business strategy protects your investment and positions your business for long-term success and competitiveness in the market. Regular upkeep should be viewed not as an expense but as an investment in your business's future and reputation.

CHAPTER 14

FINANCIAL MANAGEMENT

The Heartbeat of Your Business

Effective financial management ensures sustainability and growth in cash-based businesses such as vending machines, car washes, and laundromats. Maintaining a clear understanding of one's financial health enables strategic decision-making, optimizes operations, and drives profitability. This chapter delves into the essential aspects of financial management, including establishing solid bookkeeping practices, managing cash flow, maximizing profits, and planning for taxes and future growth. By mastering these elements, business owners can safeguard their ventures against financial pitfalls and set the stage for long-term success.

Establishing Solid Bookkeeping Practices

Accurate bookkeeping is the cornerstone of sound financial management. It systematically records and organizes all financial transactions, clearly showing your business's financial status. Accurate records are crucial for tracking sales, managing expenses, and making informed business decisions.

Tools and Systems: Choosing the right bookkeeping system depends on your business's size and complexity. Manual bookkeeping can work for small operations, but digital systems are often more efficient and reduce the risk of errors. Software solutions like QuickBooks or Xero offer features tailored to small businesses, including automated invoicing, expense tracking, and financial reporting.

Vital Financial Statements: Understanding and regularly reviewing critical financial statements is essential. The balance sheet provides a snapshot of your business's financial position at a specific time, detailing assets, liabilities, and equity. The income statement, or profit and loss (the Income Statement), shows revenue, expenses, and profit over a period. The cash flow statement tracks the inflow and outflow of cash, highlighting the business's liquidity and operational efficiency. Together, these documents offer a comprehensive view of your financial health.

Managing Cash Flow

Cash flow management ensures your business meets its financial obligations and invests in growth opportunities. It involves monitoring cash movement in and out of your business to avoid shortfalls and ensure liquidity.

Cash Flow Analysis: Regularly analyzing cash flow helps identify patterns and predict potential shortfalls. Cash flow forecasts can provide insights into future cash needs, helping you plan for seasonal fluctuations and unexpected expenses.

Strategies for Improvement: Improving cash flow can involve several strategies, such as optimizing inventory levels to prevent overstocking, adjusting pricing to reflect market demand, and reducing unnecessary expenses. For vending machines, this might mean streamlining restocking schedules. For car washes, it could involve refining service offerings to maximize revenue during peak times.

Emergency Funds: An emergency fund is essential for covering unexpected expenses or business downturns. This reserve can protect your business from financial strain and provide a safety net during tough times.

Profit Maximization Strategies

Maximizing profit involves balancing revenue growth with cost management. Here are key strategies to consider:

Pricing Strategies: Finding the optimal pricing model is crucial for maximizing revenue without deterring customers. Conduct market research to understand what your competitors charge and gauge what your target market is willing to pay. Consider offering tiered pricing or discounts for bulk purchases to attract different customer segments.

Cost Reduction: Review your expenses regularly to identify areas where you can cut costs without compromising quality. This might involve negotiating better terms with suppliers, reducing energy consumption, or streamlining operations. Implementing energy-efficient equipment in car washes can reduce utility costs, while optimizing machine usage in laundromats can lower operational expenses.

Revenue Streams: Exploring additional services or products can increase revenue. For instance, vending machines can offer premium products, car washes can introduce detailing services, and laundromats can sell laundry supplies. Upselling complementary products or services can also enhance the customer experience and boost sales.

Financial Planning and Forecasting

Effective financial planning and forecasting are essential for confidently navigating your business's future. They involve setting financial goals, budgeting, and using historical data to predict future performance.

Budgeting: A detailed budget helps guide your business decisions and aligns spending with financial goals. It should include projected revenue, operating costs, capital expenditures, and cash reserves. Regularly reviewing and adjusting your budget based on actual performance is crucial for staying on track.

Forecasting: Financial forecasting uses historical data to predict future revenue, expenses, and cash flow. It helps identify potential challenges and opportunities, allowing you to adjust your strategy proactively. Forecasts should be updated regularly to reflect changes in the market and business environment.

Adjustments and Revisions: Financial plans are not static; they should be revisited and revised as necessary. Regular financial reviews help assess the accuracy of forecasts and the effectiveness of your financial strategies. Adjusting your plans based on these reviews ensures your business remains agile and responsive to changes.

Tax Planning and Compliance

Understanding and managing your tax obligations is crucial for maintaining legal compliance and optimizing your financial position. Taxes can significantly impact your business's profitability, so planning and managing them is essential.

Understanding Tax Obligations: Cash-based businesses must diligently report all income and keep accurate records of expenses. Understanding your tax responsibilities, including income tax, sales tax, and employment tax, is vital for avoiding penalties.

Tax Saving Strategies: Several legal strategies can help minimize tax liabilities. These include tax deductions and credits for business expenses, equipment depreciation, and energy-efficient upgrades. It's advisable to consult with a tax professional to ensure you're utilizing all available options.

Staying Compliant: Staying compliant involves timely filing and payment of taxes. Maintaining organized financial records and using accounting software can simplify this process. Regularly updating yourself on tax laws and regulations helps ensure your business remains compliant and avoids fines.

- **Case Study:** FreshStart Laundromat faced financial difficulties due to poor cash flow management and a lack of strategic planning. Implementing a detailed bookkeeping system and regular financial reviews helped them better understand their financial situation. They optimized pricing strategies and reduced operational costs by negotiating better terms with suppliers and introducing energy-efficient machines.

  Additionally, FreshStart diversified its revenue streams by offering new services like wash-and-fold and dry cleaning, which appealed to a broader customer base. They also established an emergency fund to cover unexpected expenses. Through these measures, FreshStart significantly improved its cash flow and profitability, demonstrating the impact of effective financial management.

Cultivating Financial Health

Financial management is a vital component of success for cash-based businesses. Business owners can ensure financial stability and profitability by establishing solid bookkeeping practices, managing cash flow, maximizing profits, and planning for taxes and future growth. Continuous financial oversight and strategic planning enable businesses to adapt to changing market conditions and achieve long-term success. Embracing financial management as a core business strategy protects your investments and unlocks opportunities for growth and expansion. Prioritizing financial health ensures your business thrives and remains competitive in an ever-evolving market.

CHAPTER 15

EXPANDING YOUR BUSINESS

This chapter delves into strategies for growth and diversification in cash-based businesses such as vending machines, car washes, and laundromats. This chapter aims to guide entrepreneurs through the considerations and steps necessary for scaling their operations, exploring expansion models, and leveraging new market opportunities to increase revenue and brand presence.

Setting the Stage for Growth

Growth is a pivotal phase in the lifecycle of any business, providing opportunities to increase revenue, enhance market presence, and explore new avenues for innovation. For owners of cash-based businesses like vending machines, car washes, and laundromats, the expansion offers the chance to scale operations, attract new customers, and diversify offerings. However, this process requires careful planning and a strategic approach to navigate potential challenges and seize opportunities effectively. This chapter will equip you with the necessary insights and tools to assess your readiness for expansion, explore suitable growth models, and implement strategies that foster sustainable development. By the end of this chapter, you will have a comprehensive understanding of how to scale your business successfully and mitigate the risks associated with expansion.

Assessing Readiness for Expansion

Determining the right time to expand your business is crucial for ensuring successful growth. Several indicators can help you assess whether your business is primed for expansion:

1. **Consistent Profitability:** A stable profit margin indicates that your business is financially healthy and capable of sustaining additional expenses associated with expansion.
2. **Strong Customer Demand:** An increasing demand for your products or services suggests room for growth and that your offerings resonate with your target market.
3. **Operational Stability:** Efficient processes and a reliable workforce are essential for handling the complexities of expansion. Your current operations are better positioned to expand if they are stable and scalable.
4. **Market Position:** A strong market position, characterized by a loyal customer base and a recognizable brand, provides a solid foundation for entering new markets or introducing new services.

Financial considerations are critical to assessing readiness for expansion. A robust financial foundation, including sufficient cash flow, access to credit, and a clear budget for expansion activities, is essential. Reinvesting profits into the business can fund new projects, such as opening additional locations or upgrading equipment. Additionally, conducting a thorough financial analysis will help determine the feasibility and scope of your expansion plans, ensuring that they are sustainable in the long term.

Expansion Models for Cash-Based Businesses

Choosing the suitable expansion model depends on your business type and strategic objectives. Here are some potential models for different cash-based businesses:

- **Vending Machines:** Expansion can involve installing machines in new high-traffic locations such as shopping malls, office complexes, or transportation hubs. Diversifying product offerings, such as adding healthier snacks or beverages, can attract a broader customer base. Implementing advanced technologies like cashless payment systems and remote monitoring can enhance customer convenience and streamline operations.

- **Car Washes:** Car wash businesses can expand by adding new services, such as detailing, waxing, or eco-friendly washing options. Upgrading equipment to more efficient, water-saving technologies can attract environmentally conscious customers and reduce operating costs. Additionally, expanding to new locations or introducing mobile car wash services can increase market reach and customer convenience.

- **Laundromats:** For laundromats, expansion options include opening new locations, offering franchising opportunities, or diversifying services. Value-added services like dry cleaning, laundry delivery, or wash-and-fold services can differentiate your business and cater to a broader range of customer needs. Implementing a loyalty program or subscription services can also encourage repeat business and customer loyalty.

Market Analysis for New Opportunities

A thorough market analysis is essential for identifying new opportunities and ensuring that your expansion efforts align with market demand. Here are vital steps to consider:

1. **Demographic Research:** Understanding the demographics of potential new markets, including age, income levels, and lifestyle preferences, can help tailor your offerings to meet specific customer needs. This information is crucial for selecting suitable locations and targeting customer segments.

2. **Competitor Analysis:** Analyzing competitors in your target markets can provide valuable insights into their strengths, weaknesses, and market positioning. Identifying gaps in the market or areas where competitors are underperforming can reveal opportunities for your business to differentiate itself and capture market share.

3. **Customer Feedback:** Gathering feedback from your current customers can provide insights into potential new products or services that may be in demand. Understanding customer pain points and preferences can guide your expansion strategy and help ensure your new offerings are well-received.

4. **Economic and Market Trends:** Keeping abreast of economic trends, industry developments, and market forecasts can help you anticipate changes in consumer behavior and market conditions. This information is critical for making informed decisions about the timing and scope of your expansion efforts.

Diversification Strategies

Diversification is a strategy that involves expanding your business's product or service offerings to reduce risk and attract new customer segments. Here are some ways to diversify:

1. **Complementary Products or Services:** Introducing products or services that complement your existing offerings can enhance your value proposition. For example, a laundromat might add tailoring services, while a car wash could offer vehicle maintenance packages.

2. **New Customer Segments:** Expanding into new customer segments can open additional revenue streams. For instance, vending machine operators could introduce machines that offer premium or specialized products, such as organic snacks or gourmet coffee, targeting health-conscious or niche markets.

3. **Geographic Expansion:** Expanding into new geographic areas can diversify your customer base and reduce dependency on a single market. This strategy can involve opening new locations or targeting underserved areas with high potential demand.

4. **Technology Integration:** Leveraging technology can enhance your offerings and create new revenue opportunities. Implementing online booking and payment systems, loyalty apps, or customer engagement platforms can attract tech-savvy customers and improve operational efficiency.

Managing Risks in Expansion

Expansion inherently involves risks, including financial strain, market misalignment, and operational challenges. To manage these risks effectively, consider the following strategies:

Phased Expansion: A gradual, phased approach to expansion allows you to test new markets or services on a smaller scale before committing significant resources. This strategy helps mitigate financial risks and allows you to refine your offerings based on initial feedback.

Strategic Partnerships: Partnerships with other businesses can provide additional resources, expertise, and market access. For example, collaborating with local businesses or service providers can help you establish a presence in new markets more quickly and cost-effectively.

Maintaining Quality and Consistency: As you expand, it's crucial to maintain the quality of your products and services. Consistency is vital in preserving your brand reputation and customer trust. Investing in staff training, standardizing processes, and implementing quality control measures can help ensure that your expanded operations meet the same high standards as your original business.

Financial Planning and Monitoring: Careful financial planning is essential for managing the costs associated with expansion. This includes budgeting for new locations, equipment, marketing, and potential contingencies. Regular financial monitoring and analysis can help you track progress, identify potential issues early, and make informed adjustments to your strategy.

- **Case Study: Successful Business Expansion:** Consider the case of a laundromat business that successfully expanded its operations. Initially operating a single location, the business identified a growing demand for convenient laundry services in nearby neighborhoods. The owner decided to expand by opening additional locations in underserved areas. The business introduced value-added services such as dry cleaning and laundry delivery to differentiate the new locations. Additionally, they implemented a loyalty program offering regular customers discounts and perks.

  The expansion was carefully planned and executed in phases, allowing the owner to manage costs and adjust strategies based on customer feedback and market conditions. The business maintained high service standards by training staff and standardizing operational procedures. As a result, the new locations quickly gained a loyal customer base, and the business achieved a significant increase in revenue and market share. This case illustrates the importance of strategic planning, market analysis, and maintaining quality in successful business expansion.

Embracing Growth with Strategy

Expanding your business is an exciting opportunity to increase profitability, reach new markets, and enhance your brand's reputation. However, successful expansion requires careful planning, strategic decision-making, and effective risk management. By assessing your readiness, exploring suitable expansion models, conducting thorough market analysis, and considering diversification strategies, you can position your business for sustainable growth. Managing the risks associated with expansion, such as financial strain and operational challenges, is also crucial for long-term success. Ultimately, expansion is not just about growing your business but evolving to serve your customers better and meet the demands of a changing market. By staying adaptable, customer-focused, and committed to excellence, you can navigate the complexities of expansion and achieve lasting success.

CHAPTER 16

ADAPTING TO CHANGE

The Only Constant is Change

Change is inevitable in the dynamic landscape of cash-based businesses like vending machines, car washes, and laundromats. From evolving consumer preferences and technological advancements to shifts in the competitive landscape, businesses must be agile and responsive to survive and thrive. The ability to adapt quickly and effectively to these changes can be a significant determinant of success. This chapter focuses on equipping business owners with the strategies needed to anticipate, respond to, and capitalize on changes in their industry. By understanding and embracing change, businesses can protect themselves from potential disruptions and seize new opportunities for growth and innovation.

Recognizing Signs of Market Shifts

Understanding market shifts is crucial for maintaining relevance and competitiveness. There are several key indicators that businesses should monitor:

Identifying Trends: Staying informed about industry trends involves regularly reading trade publications, attending industry conferences, and participating in professional networks. Businesses should also utilize online tools and resources to track market analytics and consumer behavior patterns. This proactive approach helps spot emerging trends, such as new consumer preferences or technological advancements, that could impact your business.

Customer Feedback: Actively seeking and analyzing customer feedback is invaluable for recognizing changes in consumer behavior and expectations. This can be achieved through surveys, reviews, and direct customer interactions. Feedback helps identify areas for improvement and new opportunities, such as demand for additional services or products.

Technology and Innovation: It is essential to monitor technological developments, as new technologies can disrupt existing business models and provide opportunities for enhancement. For instance, the rise of mobile payment systems has transformed how transactions are conducted, offering more convenience for customers and businesses.

Strategies for Agile Adaptation

Adaptability is a crucial trait for businesses aiming to navigate change effectively. Here are some strategies to foster agility:

Flexibility in Operations: Develop operational processes that allow for quick adjustments. This might include flexible staffing arrangements, scalable service offerings, or adaptable supply chain logistics. A responsive infrastructure enables businesses to pivot quickly in response to market changes.

Continuous Learning and Development: Encourage a culture of learning within your organization. This can involve regular employee training on new technologies and industry best practices. Keeping your team informed and skilled ensures they can efficiently adapt to new tools and methods.

Strategic Planning with Contingencies: Prepare for various scenarios by creating contingency plans. This involves identifying potential risks, such as economic downturns or technological disruptions, and outlining actions to mitigate their impact. Regularly revisiting and updating these plans ensures they remain relevant and practical.

Leveraging Technology for Competitive Advantage

Incorporating technology into your business model can significantly enhance efficiency and customer experience:

Automation and Efficiency: Automation technologies can streamline various aspects of your business. For vending machines, this could mean automated inventory tracking and restocking. Car washes might implement automated payment and wash systems. These technologies reduce labor costs and improve service speed and accuracy.

Digital Marketing: Adapting your marketing strategies to include digital channels is essential in today's market. Utilize social media platforms, SEO, and online advertising to reach a broader audience. These tools allow targeted marketing, reaching specific demographics more effectively than traditional methods.

Data Analytics: Leveraging data analytics can provide deep insights into customer behavior and market trends. This data can inform everything from inventory management to personalized marketing campaigns. By analyzing sales data, customer feedback, and market trends, businesses can make informed decisions and anticipate changes in demand.

Diversifying Offerings to Stay Relevant

Diversification is a key strategy for staying relevant in a changing market:

Expansion of Services/Products: Consider introducing new services or products that complement your existing offerings. For example, a laundromat could expand into offering dry cleaning, or a vending machine business might add high-demand products like organic snacks. This attracts a broader customer base and mitigates risk by diversifying revenue streams.

Partnerships and Collaborations: Forming strategic partnerships can open new avenues for growth and innovation. Collaborating with local businesses, for instance, can provide cross-promotion opportunities and access to new customer segments. Partnerships can also lead to sharing resources and expertise, enhancing your business's overall capabilities.

Building a Resilient Business Model

Resilience is more than surviving changes; it's about thriving despite them. Building a resilient business involves:

Financial Resilience: Maintaining a solid financial foundation is crucial. This includes having sufficient reserves to weather economic fluctuations and carefully managing debt. Regular financial reviews and prudent budgeting are vital to ensuring long-term financial stability.

Customer-Centric Approach: Prioritizing customer satisfaction and loyalty can help insulate your business from market volatility. Happy customers are more likely to return and recommend your services to others. Regularly engaging with customers to understand their needs and preferences helps tailor your offerings and enhance their experience.

Sustainability Practices: Implementing sustainable business practices is becoming increasingly important. Whether using eco-friendly materials, reducing waste, or conserving energy, sustainability initiatives can appeal to environmentally conscious consumers and potentially lower operational costs. Additionally, they prepare your business for future regulations and market trends towards sustainability.

- **Case Study:** EcoWash Car Wash successfully navigated a significant market disruption by embracing change and innovation. Faced with increasing competition and a growing demand for eco-friendly services, EcoWash re-evaluated its business model. They invested in water recycling technology, reducing water usage by 70%, which appealed to environmentally conscious customers and significantly lowered operational costs.

  Recognizing the shift towards digital payment solutions, EcoWash integrated a mobile app that allowed customers to pay, book services, and access loyalty rewards seamlessly. They also diversified their offerings by adding premium detailing services and a subscription-based wash program, which provided steady revenue streams.

  EcoWash actively sought customer feedback to refine its services and improve customer satisfaction. It also partnered with local environmental groups, enhancing its brand's eco-friendly image and expanding its customer base.

  EcoWash weathered the competitive market through these strategic adaptations and emerged as an eco-friendly car wash sector leader. This case study underscores the importance of being proactive, customer-focused, and innovative in navigating changes.

Embracing Change as Opportunity

Adapting to change is a necessity and a powerful opportunity for growth and differentiation. Cash-based businesses can thrive in an ever-evolving market landscape by staying informed about market trends, being flexible in operations, leveraging technology, and maintaining a resilient business model. This chapter encourages business owners to view change not as a threat but as a catalyst for innovation and renewed growth. Embracing change with a proactive and strategic approach ensures your business remains relevant, competitive, and thriving in the long run. By continuously adapting and evolving, you can transform challenges into opportunities, securing your business's bright and prosperous future.

CHAPTER 17

PLANNING FOR AUTONOMY

The Value of Operational Independence

Achieving operational independence is a significant milestone for any business owner, particularly in the cash-based sectors of vending machines, car washes, and laundromats. Operational autonomy allows businesses to run smoothly with minimal daily oversight, freeing the owner to focus on strategic growth, innovation, and new ventures. This independence enhances scalability and ensures consistency in service quality and customer experience. This chapter outlines practical steps for achieving a self-sustaining business, leveraging technology, automation, and a capable team to create a streamlined, efficient operation that thrives independently.

Automating Operational Processes

Vending Machines: Automation in vending machines has revolutionized inventory management and customer transactions. Innovative technology enables real-time tracking of inventory levels, allowing for efficient restocking and reducing the likelihood of machine downtime. Remote monitoring systems can alert operators to technical issues, enabling swift resolution. More importantly, integrating digital payment systems, including mobile wallets and contactless payments, enhances convenience for customers, making them feel valued and reducing the need for cash handling.

Car Washes: Implementing automated systems in car washes significantly reduces the need for manual intervention. Automated service selection and payment processing streamline the customer experience, while highly reliable, automated wash systems ensure consistent service quality. Maintenance alerts from these systems can preemptively notify staff of potential issues, allowing for timely maintenance and minimizing operational disruptions.

Laundromats: Laundromats benefit from automated washers and dryers, which can be controlled and monitored remotely. Self-service payment systems, including app-based booking and notifications, offer unparalleled convenience and flexibility to customers. These systems can provide usage data, helping to optimize machine deployment and maintenance schedules.

Leveraging Technology for Management Efficiency

Utilizing advanced business management software can significantly streamline operations and enhance efficiency across various aspects of the business. These tools can handle everything from employee scheduling and payroll to financial and customer relationship management (CRM).

Data Analytics and AI: Leveraging data analytics and AI can provide deep insights into business performance, customer behavior, and market trends. Predictive analytics can forecast maintenance needs, optimize inventory management, and enhance customer service by anticipating needs and preferences. Using these tools, business owners can make informed decisions without being physically present, ensuring the business operates smoothly and efficiently.

Building a Self-Sustaining Team

A well-trained, empowered team is crucial for maintaining day-to-day operations with minimal owner involvement. Start by hiring individuals who align with your business values and possess the necessary skills for their roles. Comprehensive training programs should cover technical aspects, customer service standards, and emergency procedures.

Operational Manuals and Communication: Creating detailed operational manuals ensures that all team members understand their responsibilities and the standard procedures for various situations. Establishing strong communication channels, such as regular meetings and a clear reporting hierarchy, helps maintain operational consistency and address issues promptly.

Empowering Employees: Empowering your team by delegating decision-making authority for routine issues can improve efficiency and morale. Providing ongoing training and development opportunities keeps your team motivated and capable of handling new challenges, further enhancing the business's operational autonomy.

Customer Service in an Autonomous Operation

Maintaining high levels of customer service in an automated business environment is crucial for customer satisfaction and retention. Even with automation, ensuring a human touch is crucial in addressing customer needs and resolving issues.

Customer Service Kiosks and Online Feedback: Implementing customer service kiosks in physical locations or online platforms for feedback collection can facilitate communication between the business and its customers. Rapid response strategies for complaints or inquiries, such as chatbots or dedicated customer service lines, ensure issues are addressed promptly, maintaining a positive customer experience.

Continuous Improvement: Regularly reviewing customer feedback helps identify areas for improvement, even when the business operates independently of daily owner involvement. Proactively addressing common concerns and enhancing services based on feedback demonstrates a commitment to customer satisfaction, fostering loyalty and positive word-of-mouth.

Security and Safety

Security is critical for cash-based businesses, especially those operating under reduced supervision. Implementing robust security measures protects both the business and its customers.

Surveillance and Secure Payments: Installing surveillance systems with real-time monitoring and recording capabilities helps deter theft and vandalism. Secure payment technologies, including encrypted digital payment systems and secure cash handling processes, protect against fraud and theft.

Regular Security Audits: Regular security audits are essential for identifying potential vulnerabilities. These audits should cover physical security measures, digital systems, and staff training on security protocols. By proactively addressing security issues, businesses can safeguard their assets and ensure a safe environment for customers and employees.

- **Case Study:** QuickWash Car Wash is an exemplary operational autonomy model. The owners realized the need for reduced manual oversight and invested in a comprehensive automation system. This included automated service kiosks where customers could select services and make payments, reducing the need for on-site staff. The system also included automated wash equipment and an advanced monitoring system that provided real-time updates on equipment status and maintenance needs.

QuickWash utilized a sophisticated CRM system that collected customer data to enhance efficiency further, enabling personalized marketing campaigns and loyalty programs. The company also implemented a digital feedback platform, allowing customers to quickly provide feedback and report issues promptly addressed by a dedicated remote customer service team.

Investing in automation and technology allowed QuickWash to operate with minimal staff, significantly reducing labor costs while maintaining high service standards. This operational model enabled the owners to focus on expanding the business, exploring new markets, and investing in further technological innovations. QuickWash's success demonstrates the potential of a well-executed autonomy strategy, resulting in increased profitability and customer satisfaction.

Achieving Business Freedom

Achieving operational autonomy is a transformative milestone for cash-based business owners, providing the freedom to explore new opportunities and focus on strategic growth. Businesses can operate efficiently with minimal daily oversight by integrating automation, leveraging advanced technologies, building a capable team, and maintaining a strong customer service ethos. This enhances scalability and consistency and liberates owners from the demands of day-to-day management, allowing them to pursue other interests or business ventures.

However, achieving autonomy is not the final goal; it is an ongoing process of improvement and adaptation. As market conditions, technologies, and customer expectations evolve, businesses must remain agile and responsive. By continuously refining their operations and embracing innovation, business owners can ensure long-term success and maintain a competitive edge in the market. Operational independence is a powerful tool that, when achieved, opens up new horizons for growth, innovation, and personal freedom.

CHAPTER 18

CLOSING RECAP

This comprehensive guide has covered the crucial elements necessary for establishing and thriving in a cash-based business, whether in vending machines, car washes, laundromats, or other similar ventures. Each chapter has delved into specific aspects of building a successful business, offering in-depth analysis, practical advice, and actionable strategies. This closing summary aims to encapsulate the key takeaways and overarching themes, providing a cohesive reflection on the insights gathered throughout the book.

Understanding Cash-Based Businesses

The foundational chapters laid the groundwork by exploring the unique aspects of cash-based businesses. Cash-based operations offer immediate liquidity, straightforward transactions, and often simpler financial management than digital or credit-based enterprises. The advantages of such businesses include lower transaction fees, reduced dependency on financial institutions, and the appeal of tangible currency for many customers.

The Unique Appeal and Resilience: Cash-based businesses thrive in various environments where customers prefer or require physical money transactions. This includes areas with limited digital payment infrastructure or populations prioritizing privacy and budget control. Additionally, the resilience of these businesses during economic downturns or in cash-preferred communities highlights their continued relevance and potential for profitability.

Generating and Developing a Business Concept

Creating a successful cash-based business starts with a robust business concept. This involves identifying market opportunities, conducting thorough research, and refining the concept to align with market needs and the entrepreneur's strengths. A well-defined business concept clarifies the business's unique value proposition and sets the stage for detailed planning and execution.

Identifying Market Opportunities: Entrepreneurs can identify promising niches by analyzing consumer behaviors, market trends, and gaps in current offerings. Whether it's vending machines in high-traffic locations or car washes with eco-friendly options, understanding what the market lacks and how your business can fill that void is crucial.

Research and Fine-Tuning: Detailed market analysis, including demographic studies, competitive landscape assessments, and customer surveys, helps fine-tune the business concept. This process ensures the business idea is viable and competitively positioned to meet the market's demands.

Developing a Comprehensive Business Plan

A business plan is a blueprint for turning a concept into a functioning business. It encompasses several key sections, including the executive summary, company description, market analysis, organizational structure, product line, marketing strategies, financial projections, and funding requirements.

Importance of a Business Plan: The business plan is critical for securing financing, attracting investors, and guiding day-to-day operations. It forces the entrepreneur to think through every aspect of the business, anticipate challenges, and plan for growth.

Detailed Planning: By outlining the operational, financial, and marketing strategies, the business plan provides a roadmap for success. It sets specific goals, timelines, and metrics for measuring progress, ensuring that the business remains focused and aligned with its objectives.

Securing Financing and Legal Considerations

Securing the necessary funding is critical in bringing a business concept to life. This involves exploring various financing options, from traditional bank loans to venture capital and crowdfunding. Equally important are the legal considerations, including choosing the proper business structure, understanding zoning laws, and obtaining the necessary permits and licenses.

Financing Options: The book explored different avenues for securing capital, highlighting the pros and cons of each. From traditional loans and SBA loans to angel investors and crowdfunding platforms, understanding the requirements and expectations of each option is vital for making informed decisions.

Legal Framework: Navigating the legal landscape involves selecting the appropriate business structure (LLC, corporation, etc.), adhering to local zoning regulations, and ensuring compliance with health and safety standards. Proper legal planning protects the business from potential liabilities and sets a solid foundation for operations.

Design, Construction, and Operational Setup

Once the business concept is solidified and financing secured, the focus shifts to the physical and operational setup. This includes designing the facility, constructing or refurbishing spaces, purchasing equipment, and setting up daily operational systems.

Facility Design and Construction: For car washes and laundromats, the layout and design of the facility play a crucial role in operational efficiency and customer experience. The book detailed considerations for optimizing space, flow, and accessibility.

Equipment and Inventory: Selecting the right equipment and managing inventory effectively are vital for operational success. This includes choosing reliable suppliers, understanding the maintenance needs of machinery, and keeping track of inventory levels to consistently meet customer demand.

Marketing, Sales, and Customer Experience

Marketing and sales strategies are essential for attracting and retaining customers. A comprehensive marketing plan includes understanding the target market, defining a brand identity, selecting marketing channels, and setting a budget. Additionally, an excellent customer experience ensures repeat business and positive word-of-mouth referrals.

Target Market and Brand Identity: Understanding who your customers are and what they value is critical for crafting effective marketing messages. The book emphasizes the importance of a strong brand identity that resonates with your target audience and differentiates your business from competitors.

Marketing Channels and Sales Strategies: Utilizing a mix of digital and traditional marketing channels helps reach a broader audience. Whether through social media, SEO, email marketing, or local advertising, the key is to be where your customers are. Additionally, sales strategies such as promotions, loyalty programs, and upselling can drive revenue growth.

Customer Experience: Delivering a seamless and pleasant customer experience is paramount. This includes everything from the cleanliness and accessibility of the facility to the ease of transactions and responsiveness to customer inquiries. Happy customers are more likely to return and recommend your business to others.

Operations Management and Maintenance

Efficient daily operations and regular maintenance are the backbone of a successful cash-based business. This includes setting up operational systems, managing staff, maintaining equipment, and ensuring compliance with safety standards.

Operational Systems: The book discussed the importance of robust operational systems, from inventory management and cash handling to scheduling and customer service protocols. Streamlining these systems improves efficiency and reduces the likelihood of errors.

Maintenance and Upkeep: Regular maintenance of equipment and facilities ensures that the business runs smoothly and prevents costly breakdowns. The book provided checklists for daily, weekly, monthly, and annual maintenance tasks, emphasizing the importance of proactive care.

Financial Management and Planning for Growth

Financial management involves tracking income and expenses, managing cash flow, and planning for taxes. It's also about setting up systems for financial reporting, budgeting, and forecasting to make informed business decisions.

Cash Flow Management: The book highlighted the importance of maintaining a healthy cash flow, ensuring the business meets its obligations, and investing in growth opportunities. This includes effectively managing receivables and payables.

Financial Projections and Budgeting: Accurate financial projections and budgeting are essential for planning future growth and assessing the business's financial health. The book provided templates and tools for creating these financial documents.

Adapting to Change and Embracing Technology

In an ever-evolving market, the ability to adapt to change is crucial. This includes staying updated on industry trends, adopting new technologies, and continuously improving business operations.

Technological Advancements: The book explored the role of technology in enhancing efficiency and customer experience. Technology can streamline operations and provide valuable insights, from automated payment systems and inventory management software to customer engagement tools.

Adaptation and Innovation: Being adaptable means being open to change and willing to innovate. This could involve diversifying service offerings, exploring new markets, or embracing new business models. The book encouraged entrepreneurs to view change as an opportunity for growth rather than a challenge.

Planning for Autonomy and Long-Term Success

Finally, the book addresses creating a business that can operate autonomously. This involves automating processes, delegating responsibilities, and building a reliable team.

Operational Independence: Achieving operational independence allows the business owner to focus on strategic growth rather than daily management. The book discussed strategies for automating key processes and creating systems that ensure smooth operations even in the owner's absence.

Sustainability and Legacy: The ultimate goal is to build a sustainable business that generates profit and creates lasting value. This includes considering the environmental impact, contributing to the community, and planning succession or exit strategies.

Final Thoughts:

The world of cash-based businesses offers numerous opportunities for entrepreneurial success. However, it requires careful planning, diligent execution, and continuous adaptation. This book has provided a roadmap for navigating this journey, from the initial concept and business planning stages to daily operations, marketing, and beyond.

As you move forward from here, remember that the key to success lies in your commitment to learning, adapting, and striving for excellence in every aspect of your business. Whether you're just starting or looking to expand and innovate, the principles and strategies discussed in this book will serve as a valuable guide.

Thank you for visiting this business overview with me. I wish you the best of luck!

GLOSSARY

Automated Service Kiosk – A standalone device that performs services or provides goods without human intervention, commonly used in vending machines and self-service laundromats.

Break-Even Analysis – A calculation used to determine the number of products or services a business needs to sell to cover its costs, identifying the point at which revenue equals expenses.

Cash Flow – The total amount of money being transferred into and out of a business, primarily as it affects liquidity.

Contingency Planning – Preparing for unexpected events or emergencies, typically by creating a plan to manage risk and minimize impact on operations.

Customer Retention – The ability of a business to retain its customers over a specified period. High retention rates indicate a business's success in satisfying its customers' needs and preferences.

Depreciation – The reduction in the value of an asset over time, mainly due to wear and tear. It is used in accounting to allocate the cost of a tangible asset over its useful life.

Digital Payment Systems – Electronic payment methods for goods or services without cash or checks, including credit/debit cards and mobile payment apps.

E-commerce – The buying and selling of goods and services using the Internet, electronic data interchange, and other online systems. This term is relevant for cash-based businesses looking to expand their sales channels.

Foot Traffic – The number of people moving around in a particular space is vital for businesses like vending machines and laundromats in high-visibility, high-traffic areas.

Franchising – A method of business expansion in which a franchisee is granted the rights to use a franchisor's business model and brand for a specified period.

Inventory Management – The process of ordering, storing, using, and selling a company's inventory, including managing raw materials, components, and finished products.

Inventory Turnover – A ratio showing how many times a company has sold and replaced inventory during a given period, helping businesses understand the efficiency of their inventory management.

Loyalty Program – A marketing strategy designed to encourage customers to continue shopping at or using the services of a business associated with the program, often through rewards or discounts.

Market Analysis – The study of the attractiveness and dynamics of a particular market within a unique industry, including assessing the target market, competition, and demand for the product or service.

Merchant Services – A broad category of financial services intended for businesses. They include processing payments made with credit cards, debit cards, and other electronic payment methods.

Omnichannel Marketing – A multi-channel sales approach that provides customers with an integrated shopping experience, whether online from a mobile device, a laptop, or a brick-and-mortar store.

Operational Efficiency – The capability of a business to deliver products or services to its customers in the most cost-effective manner while maintaining high quality.

Point of Sale (POS) System – A combination of hardware and software allows business owners to process transactions and simplify critical day-to-day business operations.

Preventive Maintenance – Routine maintenance and inspections of equipment and facilities to prevent potential problems and ensure smooth operation.

Revenue Streams – The various sources a business earns money from selling goods or providing services.

ROI (Return on Investment) – A measure used to evaluate the efficiency or profitability of an investment, calculated by dividing net profit by the cost of the investment.

SaaS (Software as a Service) – A software distribution model in which a third-party provider hosts applications and makes them available to customers over the Internet. It is often used for business management software.

Scaling – The process of expanding a business and adjusting its operations to accommodate an increase in demand while maintaining or improving efficiency and quality.

SEO (Search Engine Optimization) – Increasing the quantity and quality of traffic to your website through organic search engine results.

Smart Technology – Advanced technological solutions, often incorporating AI or IoT, provide automation and data analytics capabilities to improve efficiency and decision-making.

Social Media Marketing – Use social media platforms to connect with your audience, build your brand, increase sales, and drive website traffic.

Sustainability Practices – Business actions and strategies prioritizing environmental conservation, social responsibility, and economic viability for long-term success.

SWOT Analysis – A strategic planning technique for identifying **S**trengths, **W**eaknesses, **O**pportunities, and **T**hreats related to business competition or project planning.

Upselling – A sales technique in which a seller induces the customer to purchase more expensive items, upgrades, or other add-ons to make a more profitable sale.

Vendor's License – A permit issued by a local or state government that authorizes a company or individual to conduct business within the government's jurisdiction.

Venture Capital – Financing that investors provide to startup companies and small businesses that are believed to have long-term growth potential.

Workflow Automation – The design, execution, and automation of processes based on workflow rules, where human tasks, data, or files are routed between people or systems based on pre-defined business rules.

APPENDICES

APPENDIX A: BUSINESS PLAN TEMPLATE

Business Plan Template for Cash-Based Business

This template provides a structured approach to creating a comprehensive business plan for your cash-based business. Each section can be tailored to reflect your unique business model, market environment, and strategic vision. Keep in mind, the more detailed and accurate your business plan, the more it will serve as a solid foundation for your business's long-term success.

Executive Summary

- **Business Name & Location:** Briefly state the name and location of your business.
- **Business Concept:** Summarize the core concept, including the cash-based model (vending machines, car wash, laundromat, etc.).
- **Financial Summary:** Highlight key financial points such as revenue forecasts, profit margins, and capital requirements.
- **Mission Statement:** Define your business's purpose and the value it aims to provide customers.
- Growth Plans: Outline your vision for growing and scaling the business.

Company Description

- **Business Background:** Detail the history and current status of your business.
- **Business Goals:** List short-term and long-term goals.
- **Target Market:** Describe your primary customers.
- **Competitive Advantage**: Explain what sets your business apart from competitors.

Market Analysis

- **Industry Overview:** Provide an industry overview, including size, growth rate, and trends.
- **Target Market Segment:** Define your target market in detail, including demographics and psychographics.
- **Competition Analysis:** Analyze direct and indirect competitors and their strengths and weaknesses.
- **Market Needs and Opportunities:** Identify the needs of your target market that your business will meet, along with potential market opportunities.

Organization and Management

- **Business Structure:** Describe the legal structure of your business (e.g., sole proprietorship, LLC).
- **Management Team:** Detail the backgrounds of key management team members.
- **Staffing Needs:** Outline current and future staffing requirements.
- **Advisory Board (if applicable):** List any advisory board members or external consultants.

Service or Product Line

- **Services or Products Offered:** Describe your business's services or products, focusing on customer value.
- **Development Stage:** Detail where your services or products are in their lifecycle (concept, development, on the market).
- **Differentiation:** Explain how your offerings stand out from the competition.

Marketing and Sales Strategy

- **Marketing Strategy:** Outline your strategy for reaching your target market, including pricing, promotions, advertising, and distribution.
- **Sales Plan:** Describe your sales strategy, team structure, and activities.
- **Customer Retention Plan:** Explain how you will retain customers and encourage repeat business.

Funding Request

- **Current Funding Requirement:** Specify the amount of funding you are requesting and the use of funds.
- **Future Funding Requirements:** Project future funding needs over the next five years.

Financial Projections

- **Profit and Loss Statement:** Summarize projected profits and losses over three to five years.
- **Balance Sheet:** Offer a snapshot of your business's financial position at a specific time.
- **Cash Flow Statement:** Show how cash is expected to flow in and out of your business.
- **Revenue Forecast:** Provide a forecast for three to five years, including assumptions.

Etcetera

- Supporting Documents: Include any additional documents that support your business plan, such as market research studies, legal documents, product pictures, or additional financial documents.

APPENDIX B: MARKETING PLAN CHECKLIST

1. Market Research

- **Identify Target Audience**: Define your ideal customer demographics (age, gender, income level, location, etc.).
- **Competitive Analysis**: Research competitors in your area and analyze their strengths and weaknesses.
- **SWOT Analysis**: Identify your business's strengths, weaknesses, opportunities, and threats.

2. Branding

- **Create a Brand Identity**: Develop a logo, color scheme, and tagline representing your business.
- **Brand Messaging**: Establish key messages that convey the benefits and values of your business.
- **Brand Consistency**: Ensure your brand identity and messaging are consistent across all marketing channels.

3. Online Presence

- **Build a Website**: Create a professional website with essential information (services, location, hours, contact details).
- **SEO Optimization**: Optimize your website for search engines to improve visibility (local SEO is crucial).
- **Google My Business**: Set up and optimize your Google My Business profile.

4. Social Media Marketing

- **Choose Platforms**: Select social media platforms where your target audience is most active (e.g., Facebook, Instagram).
- **Create Profiles**: Create business profiles with complete information and branded graphics.
- **Content Strategy**: Develop a calendar with regular posts, promotions, and engaging content.
- **Engage with Followers**: Respond promptly to comments, messages, and reviews.

5. Local Marketing

- **Flyers and Posters**: Design and distribute flyers and posters in high-traffic local areas.
- **Community Events**: Participate in or sponsor local events to increase visibility.
- **Local Partnerships**: Partner with nearby businesses for cross-promotions.

6. Promotions and Offers

- **Special Discounts**: Offer introductory discounts or loyalty programs to attract and retain customers.
- **Referral Program**: Implement a referral program to encourage word-of-mouth marketing.
- **Seasonal Promotions**: Plan promotions around holidays and local events.

7. Advertising

- **Online Ads**: Invest in online advertising (Google Ads, social media ads) targeting your local area.
- **Print Ads**: Place ads in local newspapers, magazines, and community bulletins.
- **Radio and Local TV**: Consider local radio and TV ads if the budget allows.

8. Email Marketing

- **Build an Email List**: Collect customer email addresses with their permission.
- **Email Campaigns**: Send regular newsletters with updates, promotions, and valuable content.
- **Automated Emails**: Set up automated emails for customer birthdays, anniversaries, and follow-ups.

9. Customer Engagement and Feedback

- **Customer Surveys**: Conduct surveys to gather feedback and understand customer preferences.
- **Online Reviews**: Encourage satisfied customers to leave positive reviews on Google, Yelp, and other sites.
- **Loyalty Programs**: Develop a loyalty program to reward repeat customers.

10. Monitoring and Analytics

- **Track Metrics**: Monitor key performance indicators (KPIs) such as website traffic, social media engagement, and sales.
- **Analyze Results**: Regularly analyze the effectiveness of your marketing strategies.

- **Adjust Strategies**: Be prepared to adjust your marketing plan based on performance data and feedback.

Additional Tips

- **Budget Planning**: Allocate a budget for your marketing activities and track spending.
- **Consistency**: Ensure consistent marketing efforts to maintain brand presence.
- **Professional Help**: Consider hiring a marketing professional or agency if needed.

By following this marketing plan checklist, you can effectively promote your business, attract new customers, and retain existing ones. Review and update your marketing strategies regularly to stay relevant and competitive.

APPENDIX C: LEGAL AND PERMIT CHECKLIST

1. Business Structure and Registration

- **Choose a Business Structure**: Decide if your business will be a sole proprietorship, partnership, LLC, or corporation.
- **Register Your Business Name**: If you operate under a name other than your legal business name, file a "Doing Business As" (DBA) name.
- **Obtain an EIN**: Apply for an Employer Identification Number (EIN) from the IRS for tax purposes.

2. Business Licenses and Permits

- **General Business License**: Obtain a general business license from your city or county.
- **Zoning Permits**: Ensure your business location complies with local zoning laws.
- **Health Department Permit**: Required for food trucks and businesses dealing with health and hygiene, like laundromats.
- **Fire Department Permit**: Ensure your premises meet local fire codes and safety regulations.
- **Sales Tax Permit**: Register with your state's revenue agency to collect sales tax.

3. Industry-Specific Permits

- **Car Wash:**
    - Environmental Compliance: Obtain necessary permits related to water usage and discharge.

    - Hazardous Materials Permit: If handling chemicals or other hazardous materials.

- **Laundromat:**
    - Water and Sewage Permit: Ensure compliance with local water and sewage regulations.

- **Food Truck:**
    - Mobile Vendor Permit: Obtain a permit to operate your food truck in designated areas.
    - Health Inspection: Pass regular health inspections to ensure food safety.

4. Employment Regulations

- **Workers' Compensation Insurance**: Required if you have employees.
- **Unemployment Insurance**: Register with your state's unemployment insurance program.
- **Employee Health and Safety**: Comply with OSHA standards and provide a safe working environment.

5. Financial and Tax Obligations

- **Open a Business Bank Account**: Keep your personal and business finances separate.
- **Bookkeeping System**: Set up a system for tracking income and expenses.
- **Quarterly Tax Payments**: Make estimated quarterly tax payments to the IRS if required.
- **Annual Tax Filings**: File annual tax returns at the federal, state, and local levels.

6. Additional Legal Considerations

- **Business Insurance**: Consider obtaining general liability insurance, property insurance, and other relevant coverage.
- **Trademark Registration**: Protect your brand by registering trademarks for your business name, logo, and slogans.
- **ADA Compliance**: Ensure your business is accessible to people with disabilities, as required by the Americans with Disabilities Act (ADA).

7. Record Keeping and Compliance

- **Maintain Records**: Keep detailed records of all permits, licenses, and inspections. Some permits or licenses must be located in a conspicuous place where customers can see them.
- **Renewals and Updates**: Stay on top of renewal dates for all your licenses and permits.
- **Compliance Audits**: Regularly review your compliance with all legal and regulatory requirements.
- **Stay Informed**: Laws and regulations can change, so stay informed about new legal requirements for your business.

APPENDIX D: TECHNOLOGY AND AUTOMATION GUIDE

The Impact of Technology & Automation on Cash-Based Businesses

1. Payment Processing Solutions:

- **Fact:** The adoption of digital payment systems, such as mobile payments and contactless cards, has surged globally. For example, a World Payments Report 2020 report indicated digital payments were expected to see an average annual growth rate of 21% through 2023.

- **Analysis:** For cash-based businesses, incorporating digital payment options can significantly enhance customer convenience and increase sales. Moreover, digital payments provide better transaction tracking, aiding in more accurate financial management.

2. Inventory Management Systems:

- **Fact:** Modern inventory management systems use RFID (Radio Frequency Identification) and IoT (Internet of Things) sensors for real-time inventory tracking and forecasting.

- **Analysis**: Implementing these systems can dramatically reduce the workforce required for inventory counts, decrease errors, and optimize stock levels based on predictive analytics. This improves operational efficiency and ensures that popular items are always in stock, enhancing customer satisfaction.

3. Customer Engagement Tools:

- **Fact:** Customer engagement tools like CRM (Customer Relationship Management) software have been shown to increase customer retention rates. According to Salesforce, CRM applications can help improve customer retention by as much as 27%.

- **Analysis:** For cash-based businesses, using CRM systems to manage customer interactions, feedback, and loyalty programs can lead to personalized customer experiences. This personalization fosters loyalty and can significantly increase lifetime customer value.

4. Self-Service Technologies:

- **Fact:** Self-service technologies, including kiosks and app-based ordering systems, have gained popularity across various industries. A study by Grand View Research suggested the global interactive kiosk market size was valued at USD 26.63 billion in 2020 and is expected to expand at a compound annual growth rate (CAGR) of 6.9% from 2021 to 2028.

- **Analysis:** Introducing self-service options in vending machines, car washes, and laundromats reduces labor costs and caters to the consumer preference for quick, frictionless transactions. These technologies can lead to higher throughput and revenue, especially during peak times.

5. Automation in Operations:

- **Fact:** Automation technologies, including AI-driven customer service bots and robotic maintenance systems, are becoming more accessible and affordable for small to medium-sized enterprises.

- **Analysis**: Deploying automation in operations can streamline service delivery, minimize downtime through predictive maintenance, and free up human resources for tasks that require a personal touch. While the initial investment may be significant, the long-term savings and efficiency gains can be substantial.

Integrating technology and automation into cash-based businesses offers immense potential to enhance operational efficiency and elevate the customer experience. While the implementation requires careful planning and investment, the benefits of increased convenience, optimized operations, and personalized customer engagement can lead to sustained business growth and competitiveness.

APPENDIX E: EMPLOYEE TRAINING HANDBOOK TEMPLATE

This template is a starting point for creating your employee training handbook. Customize each section to fit your business's specific needs and operations, ensuring your staff is well-equipped to contribute to its success.

Employee Training Handbook Template

Table of Contents

1. **Welcome Message**
    - Introduction from the owner/management
    - Company mission statement and values
    - Overview of the handbook's purpose

2. **Company Policies and Culture**
    - Code of Conduct
    - Dress Code
    - Equal Opportunity Employment
    - Harassment Policy

3. **Customer Service Excellence**
    - Understanding Customer Needs
    - Communication Skills
    - Handling Customer Complaints
    - Privacy and Confidentiality

4. **Operations Overview**
   - Daily Workflow and Tasks

- Opening and Closing Procedures
- Equipment Operation Guidelines
- Inventory Management

5. **Equipment Operation and Maintenance**
   - Specific Equipment Training (e.g., vending machines, washers, dryers)
   - Routine Maintenance Checks
   - Troubleshooting Common Issues

6. **Safety Protocols**
   - Workplace Safety Guidelines
   - Emergency Procedures (fire, medical emergencies, power outages)
   - Reporting Accidents and Safety Concerns

7. **Emergency Procedures**
   - Evacuation Plan
   - First Aid and CPR
   - Emergency Contact Information

8. **Health and Hygiene**
   - Personal Hygiene Standards
   - COVID-19 Protocols and Best Practices
   - Handling Cleaning Chemicals Safely

9. **Sales and Promotions**
   - Overview of Current Promotions
   - Upselling Techniques

- Loyalty Programs

10. Administrative Procedures

- Timekeeping and Payroll
- Requesting Time Off
- Reporting Issues or Concerns

11. Professional Development

- Ongoing Training Opportunities
- Feedback and Performance Reviews
- Career Advancement Paths

12. Appendices

- Quick Reference Guides
- Equipment Manuals
- Contact Information for Management

APPENDIX F: RESOURCES FOR CONTINUED LEARNING AND RESEARCH

Below is a list of resources across various formats that can offer valuable insights and foster ongoing learning for entrepreneurs in the cash-based business sector, such as vending machines, car washes, and laundromats. This compilation is designed to help you stay informed about industry trends, operational best practices, and innovative growth strategies.

Books

1. **"The Lean Startup" by Eric Ries** - Offers principles for creating a more flexible business model to help new businesses succeed.

2. **"Crushing It!: How Great Entrepreneurs Build Their Business and Influence—and How You Can, Too" by Gary Vaynerchuk** - Provides strategies for building and leveraging a personal brand for business success.

3. **"The Automatic Customer: Creating a Subscription Business in Any Industry" by John Warrillow** - Explores the benefits of subscription models and how they can be applied across various industries.

Online Courses

1. **Coursera: "Entrepreneurship Specialization"** - A series of courses that guide you through launching your own business, from the inception of an idea to getting it off the ground.

2. **Udemy: "The Essential Guide to Starting a Successful Vending Business"** - Offers practical advice on starting and scaling a vending machine business.

3. **LinkedIn Learning: "Small Business Foundations"** - Provides new small business owners with the foundational knowledge necessary to start and run a successful business.

Websites

1. **Entrepreneur.com** - This website features articles, guides, and advice on starting and running a business.

2. **Small Business Administration (SBA.gov)** - Offers comprehensive information on planning, launching, managing, and growing your business.

3. **Vending Times (vendingtimes.com)** provides news, business trends, and information about the vending machine industry.

Industry Associations

1. **National Automatic Merchandising Association (NAMA)**—This association represents the vending machine and refreshment service industry and offers resources, advocacy, and networking opportunities.

2. **International Carwash Association (ICA)** - Provides resources, education, and networking opportunities for professionals.

3. **Coin Laundry Association (CLA)**—A non-profit trade organization serving the self-service laundry industry, CLA offers business tools, education, and advocacy.

Additional Resources

1. **Google My Business** is a free tool for managing your online presence across Google, including search and maps. It helps local businesses attract and retain customers.

2. **SCORE (score.org)** - Offers free business mentoring and education as a resource partner of the U.S. Small Business Administration.

3. **Meetup (meetup.com)** helps users find and join local entrepreneur groups and events and network with fellow business owners.

This list is not exhaustive but provides a solid foundation for cash-based entrepreneurs to begin or continue their educational journey. As industries evolve, always look for new and relevant resources.

Made in United States
Troutdale, OR
11/03/2026

56844713R00077